INTRODUCING
PEOPLE
OF THE
BIBLE
VOLUME TWO

Also by John Phillips

Exploring Genesis
Exploring the Psalms
Exploring the Song of Solomon
Exploring the Book of Daniel
(by John Phillips and Jerry Vines)
Exploring the Gospels: John
Exploring Acts
Exploring Romans
Exploring Ephesians
Exploring Hebrews
Exploring Revelation

Exploring the Future
Exploring the Scriptures
Exploring the World of the Jew
Bible Explorer's Guide

Introducing People of the Bible, Volume 1

INTRODUCING

PEOPLE

OF THE

BIBLE

VOLUME TWO

JOHN PHILLIPS

LOIZEAUX BROTHERS
Neptune, New Jersey

INTRODUCING PEOPLE OF THE BIBLE, VOLUME 2
© 1993 by John Phillips

A Publication of Loizeaux Brothers, Inc.

A Nonprofit Organization Devoted to the Lord's Work
and to the Spread of His Truth.

*All Scripture quotations, unless otherwise noted, are
from the King James version.*

*Library of Congress Cataloging-in-Publication Data
(Revised for vol. 2)*

*Phillips, John, 1927–
Introducing people of the Bible.
1. Bible—Biography.   I. Title.
BS571.P52   1991   220.9'2 [B]   91–39819
ISBN 0-87213-628-0*

Printed in the United States of America

10 9 8 7 6 5 4 3 2 1

Contents

1
Enoch,
the Holiest Saint

Genesis 5:18-24; Hebrews 11:5-6; Jude 14-15

I. SURROUNDING GLOOM
   A. Socially It Was an Age of Permissiveness
   B. Scientifically It Was an Age of Progressiveness
   C. Spiritually It Was an Age of Presumptuousness
II. SAVING GRACE
III. SIMPLE GOODNESS
IV. SUDDEN GLORY

E noch appears only three times on the sacred page. The
brief summary we have of his history, however, is
freighted with significance. We read of him in Genesis
5:18-24, where we are told of his birth, his children, his walk
with God, and his rapture to Heaven. We read of Enoch in
Hebrews 11:5, where we are told that he pleased God and was
translated to Heaven. We read of him in Jude 14-15, where we
learn that he preached to the ungodly of his day, warning them

of the Lord's coming in judgment. And that is all. But in these fleeting references, we have in a thumbnail biographical sketch the essence of the rapture.

Enoch and Noah stand out in the book of Genesis as archetypes of the last days. Enoch typifies the saints who will be caught away bodily to Heaven before the end-time judgments begin. That is, he symbolizes the church. Noah typifies those who will go through the storm but be preserved by God and emerge safely on the other side of judgment to inaugurate a new dispensation. In other words, Noah symbolizes Israel and the tribulation saints, who will be protected by the power of God and land safely on the millennial shore.

There were two kinds of people on the earth in the days of Enoch: the descendants of Cain and the descendants of Seth. The Bible records Cain's kind in Genesis 4 and Seth's kind in Genesis 5. Cain's kind lived for this world; Seth's kind lived for the world to come. To give us a record of Cain's kind of people, the Holy Spirit takes us into the market. He gives us a glimpse of great cities filled with the fruits of art, science, and industry—cities bursting with activity, excitement, and the everyday business of life. To give us a record of Seth's kind, the Holy Spirit takes us, of all places, into the morgue. All the way through Genesis 5 we hear the tolling of the bell: "And he died. . . . and he died. . . . and he died." It is God proving the devil a liar. The devil had said, "Ye shall not surely die" (3:4). God says, "He died. . . . he died. . . . he died."

The Holy Spirit says *twice* of each of the godly people in the line of Seth that he *lived:* "He lived. . . . he lived. . . . he died." He does not say the same of the Cainites. Each Sethite experienced a birth and another birth. Each lived and lived on, living again on the farther side of a new birth. From the standpoint of Heaven, it was the Sethites who lived, not the Cainites.

In recording the line of the Cainites, the Holy Spirit notes their worldly accomplishments but does not say that they lived. No doubt the Cainites, with their burgeoning civilization, their hot-beat music, their business enterprises, and their scientific discoveries, thought they were living, but God does not say so. He says it was the quiet, unassuming Sethites—those who contributed nothing to the world's pleasure, prosperity, or power—who really lived.

The Holy Spirit also says that the Sethites died. One would have expected Him to record the deaths of the godless Cainites, since "the wages of sin is death" (Romans 6:23). But He ignores their deaths and records instead the deaths of the children of Seth. The reason is that "precious in the sight of the Lord is the death of his saints" (Psalm 116:15). For the child of God, death is not the end. All death does is swing wide the gates of glory. Death lifted the Sethites above the sordid sins and the sadness of the cities of men. Death placed them in that great city where the streets are paved with gold, where time is not counted by years, and where Christ sits at the right hand of God.

The roll call of the dead in Genesis 5 continues until the introduction of Enoch, the seventh from Adam (Jude 14) in the godly line of Seth. In Genesis 5:24 we read about something quite different from death. Instead of a tomb there is a translation! God did something new on earth, something He had never done before but most certainly intends to do again. He reached down and took a man bodily into Heaven. Enoch went home, body and all, without having to pass through death.

In this first character study we will be considering this man Enoch and the lessons of his life. Enoch was a candidate for rapture, and as such is of surpassing interest to us who live in the closing moments of the church age. When we think of Enoch, we think of four things. We think of *surrounding gloom,* for he lived in a dark day. We think of *saving grace,* for there came a time when God met Enoch and saved him. We think of *simple goodness* because he walked with God in the midst of a pornographic society. And we think of *sudden glory,* for one moment Enoch was here on earth and the next moment he was there in the glory land, walking in his own body down the streets of gold.

I. SURROUNDING GLOOM

Enoch lived at the beginning of the climactic events that precipitated the flood. When Enoch was born, Adam was 622 years old. Adam had lived long enough to see what "one man's disobedience" (Romans 5:19) had done to the human race. He must have been the saddest man who ever lived. When Enoch was born, Seth—the founder of the godly line—was 492. Enoch's father Jared was 162, a young man according to the standard of the times. In other words, Enoch lived alongside Adam for 308 years and alongside the other patriarchs all his life. Yet even the presence of such notable "salt" was not sufficient to arrest the corruption of the age.

One place on the Niagara river is called "the point of no return." Someone who falls into the river below that point will go right over the precipice of the falls into the boiling caldron at the bottom. Enoch was born at a point of no return. The rising tides of wickedness were such that nothing could stop the world from falling into the judgment waters of the flood. God's Spirit was about to cease His striving with men; judgment was on the way. Enoch was raptured to Heaven just seventy years before Noah was born. Every sign would seem to suggest that today we stand where Enoch stood in his day—on the verge of rapture.

Enoch lived in an age of permissiveness, progressiveness, and presumptuousness.

A. Socially It Was an Age of Permissiveness

In Enoch's day people did "their own thing." Society imposed no restraints on crime and lawlessness flourished. Immorality was an accepted way of life, marriage a mere matter of convenience. Polygamy was an acceptable lifestyle.

The Holy Spirit says that the thoughts of men's hearts were "only evil continually" (Genesis 6:5). Lamech, seventh from Adam in the line of Cain, openly espoused the doctrine of permissiveness. He shook his fist in the face of God and told

Him to stay out of his life. Just as godliness had climaxed in
Enoch, seventh from Adam in the godly line of Seth, so
godlessness had climaxed in Lamech, seventh from Adam in
the godless line of Cain. The wheat and the tares ripened
together. As saintliness ripened for rapture, so sinfulness
ripened for wrath.

B. Scientifically It Was an Age of Progressiveness

In Enoch's day people were wresting secrets from nature
and making tremendous strides in science, engineering, and
technology. Men had discovered the art of smelting, and the
world had come through the antediluvian equivalent of an
industrial revolution. Driven out of Eden, men were creating an
artificial paradise based on science and technology. Great cities
were flourishing, the exploding world population was becoming increasingly urban, and social sophistication was replacing
the simplicity of earlier times.

C. Spiritually It Was an Age of Presumptuousness

Cain had corrupted the faith that God had delivered to
Adam—the faith for which the martyr Abel had been prepared
to shed his blood—into a social gospel. Believers made little
or no impact on society. Truth still lingered in the Sethite family;
fathers handed down the torch of testimony to their sons.
Cainite civilization, however, largely ignored the Sethites.

Secularism and spiritism marked the spiritual climate of
the age. Society was utterly *secularistic,* totally preoccupied
with the good things of this life. The world was materialistic.
People were absorbed with the necessities of life (eating and
drinking) and the niceties of life (marrying and giving in
marriage) and were blind to spiritual realities. As Jesus put it,
they "knew not until the flood came, and took them all away"
(Matthew 24:39). It never occurred to them that God might
have something to say to them.

Along with secularism, *spiritism* flourished. People were
tampering with the forbidden secrets of the occult. There

seems to have been a diabolical breakthrough. Men had learned the deep things of Satan. Fallen angelic beings were mingling with the daughters of men and producing a hybrid demon progeny on the earth (Genesis 6:4). The mythology of the ancient world derived from this period of time. The love stories of the gods, so prominent in Greek religion, had their roots in this age. Satanism, the ultimate feature of the apostasy of Enoch's day, necessitated the holocaust of the flood. The race was corrupted beyond recall.[1]

Such was the gloom surrounding Enoch's generation. He lived in an age that was ripening fast for judgment, very much like the age in which we live.

Some years ago journalist Ed Sanders wrote a book about his investigation of the murders committed by the Manson "family." Charles Manson was a hippie, a Satanist, a car thief, a cult leader, and a sex maniac. He gathered around him a group of about twenty girls and a few young men who became so committed to him that they were willing to do anything, anywhere, any time for him. They became extensions of his personality and will.

In the introduction to his book Sanders described the lengths to which he was prepared to go to obtain accurate information on the "family."[2] He posed as a pornography dealer, a Satanist, and a psychopathic maniac. He investigated occult societies in Los Angeles, paying special attention to Satanists, to people who practice pain magic, and to occult groups who drink dog's blood, hang up rotting goats' heads in their kitchens, and rent corpses for their parties. He met people who commit human sacrifice and who told him ghastly tales of sacrificial rituals performed on the mountains and beaches of California. He abandoned some of his plans because the areas he set out to investigate were too dangerous.

While reading that introduction, I had to remind myself constantly that Sanders was not describing David Livingstone's Africa. He was not describing the upper reaches of the Amazon. He was describing twentieth-century America. Truly we live amid surrounding gloom. We live where Enoch lived, in a world that is plunging into the same seething caldron of sin that in all ages calls down God's judgment on society.

II. SAVING GRACE

Enoch, we are told, "walked with God after he begat Methuselah" (Genesis 5:22). Methuselah was born when Enoch was sixty-five years old. During his first sixty-five years Enoch lived an ordinary life. He may not have committed the same kinds of sin that the Cainites committed, but he was just as lost as the wildest and worst of them. He was born of Adam's ruined race. His father was a godly man and his grandfather was a godly man. Enoch stood in succession to a long line of godly men, but that did not make Enoch godly. He was lost and needed to experience saving grace.

When Enoch was sixty-five years old, he had an encounter with the living God that changed his life. From that moment on he began to walk with God. Since God does not walk the paths of sin, we know that Enoch came to a turning point in his life. He had what we would call a conversion experience. It changed the whole direction of his life. That is what genuine conversion is—a meeting with Christ that gives a new direction to life. Instead of going our own way, we begin to go His way.

Many centuries after Enoch's day the prophet Amos, speaking to another apostate age, threw down the challenge: "Can two walk together, except they be agreed?" (Amos 3:3) When the Bible says that Enoch walked with God, it means that he and God were in agreement—in agreement about the way he spent his time, about the way he spent his money, about the way he ran his business, about the way he treated his family, about the way he supported his place of worship. Enoch stumbled at first, no doubt, but then walked in this new life with ever-increasing confidence until he strode out along the upward way. Enoch walked with God.

III. SIMPLE GOODNESS

Walking with God resulted in a twofold testimony. First Enoch had *a testimony Godward.* According to Hebrews 11:5 Enoch "had this testimony, that he pleased God." Crossing the great divide that separates the Old Testament from the New, we meet another man who had the testimony that He pleased God. His name was Jesus. As God watched His Son tread these scenes of time, He opened Heaven and declared, "This is my beloved Son, in whom I am well pleased" (Matthew 3:17). So when we read that Enoch and Jesus had the selfsame testimony, we can only conclude that Enoch—in the pornographic society of his day—lived like Jesus lived.

Enoch had *a testimony manward* too. Jude 14-15 tells us that he preached to the wicked people among whom he lived about the coming of Christ in judgment: "Behold, the Lord cometh with ten thousands of his saints, To execute judgment upon all." Enoch's vision of the Lord's coming leaped over a thousand years to the flood, over another two-and-a-half millennia to Bethlehem and the first coming of Christ, and over another two thousand years of the age of grace to our day when we are looking for the rapture and the second coming of Christ.

Enoch saw the Lord coming "with ten thousands of his saints." Before the Lord comes *with* His saints, He has to come *for* His saints. The rapture of the church has to take place before Christ returns to reign. Enoch did not envision the coming of Christ for His saints; he participated in it! He was caught away before the catastrophe of the flood, just as we will be caught away prior to the judgments of the last days. Each day that Enoch lived he came closer to that surprise event, just as each day we live we come closer to the rapture of the church. Whole books have been written about events that must take place before the Lord comes with His saints. Not a chapter, page, paragraph, or single line can be written about events that must happen before the Lord comes for His saints. The rapture is imminent. It is the next item on the prophetic program. It could take place at any moment.

IV. SUDDEN GLORY

One moment Enoch was here; the next moment he was gone. Adam died. Abel died. Seth died. One by one each of the saints of God listed in Genesis 5 died—except Enoch. He "was translated that he should not see death" (Hebrews 11:5).

Genesis 5:24 says of Enoch that "he was not." Hebrews 11:5 says he "was not *found*" (italics added). In other words, people missed him and went looking for him. They suddenly realized the capital value of a man who knew how to walk with God. Now Enoch was gone and a tremendous sense of loss swept through his home, his community, his business, and the place where he met with the people of God. Enoch was sought in vain. God had called him home to Heaven by way of the rapture. Judgment was now inevitable and was already bearing down on the world.

One of these days God is going to reach down and take home to Heaven not just a champion, but a church! Millions of people are going to be missing—mysteriously and unmistakably gone from this planet. Parents will look for their children who have vanished without a trace. Young people will look for their parents. Husbands will look for their wives. Wives will look for their husbands in vain. But after the initial shock the world will continue on its way, and a new surge of every form of wickedness will instantly become evident.

Two kinds of people will be called home when the Lord appears in the air. Some will still be alive when He comes. As they go up, clothed instantly with immortality, they will sing, "O death, where is thy sting?" Others who through the ages have died trusting in Jesus—those whose mortal remains have been buried and returned to the dust—will also rise. Changed, transformed, and immortal, they will come bounding out of their graves singing, "O grave, where is thy victory?" (1 Corinthians 15:55) What a chorus that will be.

Some time ago, while driving through Atlanta, I listened to a man preaching on the radio. He had been talking about the second coming of Christ and had been recounting some signs of the times. He then turned his attention to Paul's assurance that the Lord will descend from Heaven with a shout, with the voice of the archangel, and with the trump of God. "Brethren," he said, "the coming of Christ for His own is so close today that I have *stopped looking for the signs* and I have *started listening for the sounds.*" We can say a hearty amen to that!

1. See John Phillips, *Exploring Genesis* (Neptune, NJ: Loizeaux, 1980) 78-80.
2. Ed Sanders, *The Family* (New York: Avon, 1972)

2
Caleb,
the Staunchest Fighter

Joshua 14:6-15

I. THE GREAT DECISION
   IN THE WAKING YEARS OF LIFE
II. THE GREAT DEDICATION
   IN THE WORKING YEARS OF LIFE
III. THE GREAT DETERMINATION
   IN THE WEAKER YEARS OF LIFE

Caleb was a very old man. The Jews divided old age into three stages: from sixty to seventy was "the commencement of old age"; from seventy to eighty was "hoary-headed age"; and a man over eighty was said to be "well stricken in years." Caleb was eighty-five. About the time most of us have been on Social Security for twenty years and are thinking of going into a nursing home, Caleb was thinking of conquering a mountain. "Give me this mountain," he said (Joshua 14:12).

We are going to study the story of Caleb, a man who finished well. We will divide his story into three parts: *the great decision* that marked the waking years of his life; *the great dedication* that marked the working years of his life; and *the great determination* that marked the weaker years of his life.

It is a great thing to finish well. The apostle Paul told us that he had a constant fear of finishing up his life as a wicked old man on one of God's rubbish heaps, of being "a castaway" (1 Corinthians 9:27). That is a healthy fear. Many people have started well but not finished well. Solomon started well, King Saul started well, Lot started well, and Demas started well. The Bible is strewn with the wreckage of men like them who started well but ended as failures.

We may become weak in body, but the important thing is to be strong in spirit, strong enough to say to God, "Give me this mountain." Let the novice and the tenderfoot be content with an easy path. Let us take on a mountain before we die. Let us determine to tackle giants.

When he was seventy-five, Abraham left Ur of the Chaldees to become the father of all believers and to become known in Heaven as the friend of God. At the age of eighty Moses left shepherding Jethro's flocks to become the "Abraham Lincoln" of his day and the greatest lawgiver of all time. And when Caleb was eighty-five, he set out to take on the sons of Anak, to give the devil and his brood a thrashing such as they had never experienced, and to leave the world a much cleaner place.

I. THE GREAT DECISION
IN THE WAKING YEARS OF LIFE

It is never too late to start tackling giants, but it is better to start young. Caleb started young, persevered in the perilous middle-age years, and finished well. At a comparatively young age he was filled with the vision of *a new Lord, a new life,* and *a new land.*

Caleb was born a slave in the land of Egypt. He knew the wretchedness, the defeat, and the constant humiliation of bondage. He knew the bite of the taskmaster's lash and the ever-present threat of death. He longed for a savior, for someone to come and lead him into a new dimension of living. He was tired of being kicked, cursed, beaten, and bullied. He was tired of being treated like an animal.

Then one day he made a great discovery. He did not have a Bible, but he did have the book of Genesis burned into his conscience by the verbal tradition of his people. He knew the stories of Abraham and Isaac and Jacob and Joseph. He knew the Abrahamic covenant by heart. Suddenly he remembered something God said to Abraham.

We can imagine Caleb perspiring profusely, toiling under a load of fresh-dried bricks, and stopping abruptly in his tracks when the great idea occurs to him. Oblivious of the taskmaster's whip and heedless of the savage curses of his particular Egyptian bully, Caleb is working something out in his mind. The idea is little short of an inspiration from Heaven. He is remembering that many centuries ago God said that Abraham's seed would be strangers in a foreign land; they would be oppressed for four hundred years but would find their freedom in the fourth generation.

There had been a stir among the Hebrew slaves in Goshen about the time Caleb was born. He remembered his parents talking about it. A man named Moses, the adopted son of pharaoh's daughter, had thrown in his lot with the Hebrew slaves. He had come as their kinsman-redeemer, but they had rejected him. But it was the fourth generation—Levi, Kohath, Amram, Moses—and Moses had to be coming back! Caleb's generation had to be the generation that would witness the return of the kinsman-redeemer. Hallelujah! From now on a new Lord filled his vision.

II. THE GREAT DEDICATION
IN THE WORKING YEARS OF LIFE

Moses did return, armed with might and miracle. Water turned into blood. Dust turned into lice. Hail and fire fell from the sky. Egypt swarmed with frogs, flies, and locusts. Darkness and death visited the land. Caleb learned what it meant to be put under the shelter of the blood (Exodus 12:12-13). He was baptized unto Moses in the cloud and in the sea (1 Corinthians 10:1-2). Caleb gathered with God's redeemed people around the table in the wilderness. He went to Sinai and learned how to order his life. He drank from the riven rock and feasted on bread from heaven (10:3-4).

Then Caleb came to Kadesh-barnea where, as one of the twelve spies, he had a taste of the promised land, a taste of all that awaited him in Canaan. One taste of the fruits of Canaan spoiled his appetite for the onions, leeks, and garlic of Egypt. After that foretaste, the vision of *a new land* and *a new life* in Canaan drew him onward.

In the majority report the ten carnal spies told terrifying tales of great fenced cities. In Canaan the ten spies had seen the sons of Anak—a race of giants—and had seen themselves as grasshoppers. But not Caleb! When others saw giants, Caleb saw God. When others saw cities walled up to heaven, Caleb saw cities reduced to rubble. When others saw a dangerous, dreadful, diabolical foe, Caleb saw only a defeated foe. When others only saw foes, Caleb saw fruit.

When others looked at the problems, Caleb looked at the promises. Had not Joseph said, "God will surely visit you, and bring you out of this land unto the land which he sware to Abraham, to Isaac, and to Jacob" (Genesis 50:24)? When so many of his fellow believers grumbled, complained, fretted, found fault, and fought among themselves, Caleb followed the Lord.

When he was eighty-five years old, Caleb could look back over the years and give this testimony to Joshua: "I have wholly followed the Lord."

Caleb had had to learn the lesson of positively trusting God early in life. The name *Caleb* means "dog"! His father Jephunneh seems to have had a bitter sense of humor. Having heard that a son had been born to him in that ghetto in Goshen, he may have jibed: "A son? What's the use of a son? Call him "dog" for all I care. It's a dog's life he'll have down here in Egypt."

The story is told of a man who went to a psychiatrist and said, "I have this terrible feeling that I'm a dog." The psychiatrist said, "How long has this been going on?" The man said, "Ever since I was a puppy."

That is how long the identification had been going on for Caleb—except he made up his mind that he was going to glory in that insulting name and make it a badge of honor. *If I'm going to be called "dog,"* he decided, *then I'll be the best dog around.*

When my son was quite young he decided he wanted a dog. He heard about a neighbor whose cocker spaniel had just had pups, and my son wanted to know if he could have one. "They are only fifty dollars each," he said. His mother, who didn't want a dog, said, "You can have a dog when you can afford to buy one." She thought she had settled the matter. However, another neighbor had a little business making flea collars, and our boy got friendly with his boy. The two of them went to work making flea collars, and within two weeks my son came home with a cocker spaniel pup.

There was something special about that dog. My son bought it, my wife fed it, my daughters exercised it, and yet that dog was crazy about me! When I'd get home late at night after preaching out of town, I'd often find the house dark and silent. Everyone else was in bed, but that dog would wait up for me. He'd wag his tail, bounce around, and show every sign of enthusiasm because the master of the house was home.

Caleb decided if he was going to be a dog, he'd be that kind of dog. He'd let his Master in Heaven know how much he loved Him.

A good dog knows who its master is. It follows hard at its master's heels and doesn't run off on expeditions of its own. It goes where the master goes and does what it is told to do. It follows in the master's steps all the time.

Caleb decided that if he was going to be called "dog," he'd be the Lord's dog. He would wholly follow the Lord. He'd be the best dog the Master ever had. Later, looking back over some sixty years, he could say that the controlling principle of his life had been absolute loyalty to the living God and to the kinsman-redeemer He had sent.

Caleb followed the Lord fully, faithfully, and fearlessly—even when people took up stones to throw at him for his stand. No foe could daunt him. No fear could haunt him. Nobody could turn him aside. He was going where God was going, and he would be hard at His heels wherever that might be. As it turned out, following the Lord involved forty years of wandering here, there, and everywhere, up and down a howling wasteland. No matter! If God was going there, that was where Caleb was going. All the time he was wandering in the wilderness he was living by faith in Canaan.

III. THE GREAT DETERMINATION
IN THE WEAKER YEARS OF LIFE

Caleb was determined to end his life well. When we think of Caleb we should think of the mighty Amazon. Boisterous in its youth, this river is a settled, invincible, and steady flow in its old age.

The Amazon starts three miles high in the snow-swept Andes of Peru. At the source the river is only seventy miles from the Pacific ocean, but it travels nearly four thousand miles across the width of a continent toward the Atlantic. In the beginning a tiny trickle tumbles down a mountain and begins a long, eventful journey to the ocean. The stream takes its time and as it wends its way, it draws the water of two hundred other streams and brooks into its embrace until it is a full-fledged river. The Amazon churns through mountain passes, bursts with explosive force into the green wall of the jungle below, and becomes an inland sea, draining nearly half of South America—an area equal to two-thirds of the United States. At the mouth the banks stand ninety miles apart. When the Amazon reaches the end of its adventurous journey, it refuses to die. The power and drive of the river are so great that it floods the ocean with fresh water up to one hundred miles offshore. Indeed the current can still be seen two hundred miles out to sea.

Caleb was like the Amazon. At the ripe age of eighty-five he refused to consider for a moment that he had reached beyond hoary-headed age and was now well stricken in years. "Well stricken in nothing," Caleb would say. "Me? I'm ready to tackle a mountain. Me retire? Go to Florida and play golf? Not me! Give me an untamed mountain. Up to now I've just been in training. Now I'm ready to start."

By the time George Muller reached seventy he had already accomplished more than a half dozen ordinary men could accomplish in their combined lifetimes. His work with orphans had begun with a tiny trickle—some small change, three dishes, twenty-eight plates, three basins, one jug, four mugs, three saltstands, one grater, four knives, and five forks. But the work had grown and grown. Eventually there were five large buildings and a considerable staff and 2,050 boys and girls in his orphanages.

Through the years some ten thousand homeless boys and girls had been housed, fed, clothed, educated, and settled in gainful employment. Muller had given away large sums of money to help Sunday schools and day schools at home and abroad. He had circulated nearly two million Bibles and Testaments. He had distributed over three million books and tracts. It would be a hopeless task to try to calculate the cost of all this. The figures given in pounds sterling would have to be multiplied by the rate of exchange and then by an inflation factor representing the difference between the purchasing power of a dollar 150 years ago and a dollar today. The dollar amount would be astronomical; yet Muller, a poor man, obtained every penny by asking God for it. He did not ask anyone else for money.

At the age of seventy Muller decided the time had come for a change. When most of us would be thinking of a retirement home, he looked for a global parish. During the first eight years after his conversion he had offered himself as a candidate for the mission field five times, but he had always been turned down. (One wonders about the spiritual insight of the mission boards that rejected such a man.) Now Muller decided he had no need for a mission board and started out on his own. He traveled some two hundred thousand miles (long before the age of the airplane), visited forty-two countries, and preached at least six thousand times. For over seventeen years he was a living demonstration to hundreds of thousands of people that "God . . . is, and that he is a rewarder of them that diligently seek him" (Hebrews 11:6).

At ninety-one Muller said: "I am very near the end of my earthly pilgrimage. Still, I am able to work every day, and all day too. I preach five or six times a week besides. I am unspeakably happy."

That was George Muller—a veritable Amazon of a man. And that, too, was Caleb. At eighty-five he could say: "I am as strong this day as I was in the day that Moses sent me: as my strength was then, even so is my strength now, for war. . . . Now therefore give me this mountain" (Joshua 14:11-12).

. Caleb knew the fight ahead would be arduous, for that mountain would have to be stormed. It would be an uphill fight all the way. He knew it would be tedious, for the great fenced cities were walled up to heaven. They would have to be taken by long and stubborn siege. He knew the fight would be dangerous, for the sons of Anak lived there. But Caleb was not deterred. He had his eye on the land. He had been thinking of the new land ever since he was a slave in Egypt, in the house of bondage. What he wanted was an abundant entrance into that land. As Johnson Oatman, Jr., put it:

I want to live above the world,
Tho Satan's darts at me are hurled;
For faith has caught the joyful sound,
The song of saints on higher ground.

That was Caleb's battle cry. "If so be the Lord will be with me, then I shall be able to drive them out as the Lord said" (Joshua 14:12). That was Caleb's victorious philosophy of life. He was counting on the Lord's *presence.* He was counting on the Lord's *power.* He was counting on the Lord's *promise.* He was an old dog now. He looked into the face of his Master and said, "If You're going up this mountain, I'm coming too." Faithful. Reliable. Steady. That was Caleb all the way through.

Years ago Alan Redpath, a former pastor of Moody Church, was crossing the Atlantic on the *Queen Elizabeth,* the world's largest liner. A smudge of smoke on the far horizon eventually resolved itself into the SS *United States,* the world's fastest liner. As the fast ship drew alongside and passed Redpath's ship, the skipper of the *United States* flashed a message to the skipper of the *Queen Elizabeth:* "You're very beautiful but you're very slow." Back came the answer: "It is not meet for the royal lady to keep fast company!"

Alan got to know the *Queen Elizabeth's* chief engineer, who took him down to see the engines, the four giant boilers, and the two enormous propeller shafts going out to the blades. The shafts were 450 feet long (150 yards of solid steel). Alan and the engineer could hear the thrash of four giant propellers driving all 82,000 tons of that mighty floating hotel across the Atlantic.

Alan said, "I suppose those propellers must be going round at an enormous rate."

"It's evident that you are no engineer," said the chief. "I could get those propellers going around so fast they'd simply dig a hole in the water. The ship would slow down and stop— with the propellers going at full speed." He paused. "I have forty-eight engineers on this ship, and they are continually calculating the ratio between revolutions per minute in the engine room and steadiness at the point of drive."

That was the secret of that great ship—steadiness at the point of drive. That was the secret of Caleb's life. He wholly followed the Lord. That is also the secret of a productive Christian life.

3
Saul,
the Worst Fool

1 Samuel 26:21

I. HOW DESPERATELY HE REQUIRED DAVID

II. HOW DISDAINFULLY HE RIDICULED DAVID

III. HOW DEEPLY HE RESENTED DAVID

IV. HOW DELIBERATELY HE REJECTED DAVID

V. HOW DREADFULLY HE REPUDIATED DAVID

K ing Saul is an enigma. He was called of God, anointed with holy oil, given another heart, and numbered among the prophets, but he was as lost as a pagan. The explanation of his life becomes clear, however, the moment we look at him in his relationship with David. What did Saul do with David? What did David do with Saul? Those are searching questions.

We can understand other puzzling people too if we ask questions about their relationship with Christ. What did this man or that woman do with Jesus? What will Jesus do with them? Such questions put each of us into final focus.

As we look at King Saul in his relationship with David, we will consider how Saul required, ridiculed, resented, rejected, and repudiated David.

I. HOW DESPERATELY HE REQUIRED DAVID

Something was missing in Saul's life from the very start. The problem really began with Kish, the father of Saul. First Samuel 3:20 tells us that "all Israel from Dan even to Beersheba knew that Samuel was established to be a prophet of the Lord"—all Israel, that is, except Kish and Saul, or so it seems.

Saul was an impressive man. He was the kind of man at whom people would take a second and a longer look. But he was ignorant concerning spiritual things. His own servant knew the things of God better than he (1 Samuel 9:6). The servant, said Alexander Whyte, would rush off to sit at Samuel's feet whenever he had a holiday.

Samuel had grown gray in the service of God. He had traveled regularly from place to place for many long years, earnestly teaching people about God. Everybody knew Samuel. Saul's servant knew Samuel, but Saul did not recognize the prophet even when face to face with the man of God. "Then Saul drew near to Samuel in the gate, and said, Tell me, I pray thee, where the seer's house is. And Samuel answered Saul, and said, I am the seer" (1 Samuel 9:18-19). This unfamiliarity with the old prophet indicates an area of desperate need in Saul's life.

After he became king, Saul remained ignorant of spiritual things. First Samuel 10:9 says that God gave Saul another heart, but we must read that verse in context. We can only judge a man's heart by what comes out of it. God did not give Saul a *regenerated* heart. That is obvious from the whole tenor of his life. God gave Saul a *royal* heart. God never calls a man to do a task without giving him what he needs to do it. If Saul was to be king, even though he was the choice of a rebellious people (1 Samuel 8:7,19), God would give him the heart of a king. God would give him the ability to think and act like a king. (Not that Saul availed himself of the ability very often—but he had it.)

As for Saul's gift of prophecy (1 Samuel 10:10), that had all the marks of excess that characterize many who claim to have the sign gifts today. Speaking with ecstatic utterance does not prove one to be a true child of God. Pagans can speak in tongues. African witch doctors can speak in tongues and prophesy. People can speak in tongues and prophesy to the satisfaction of the charismatic community without being born-again.

Prophecy is only sounding brass and tinkling cymbal if it is divorced from love (1 Corinthians 13:1-2). Saul had little love for anyone and no love at all for David. Possessing the gift of prophecy does not prove anything. The pagan psychic Balaam prophesied—and truly (Numbers 22–24). The godless self-seeking opportunist, Caiaphas, prophesied—and truly (John 11:49-53). We must not evaluate Saul's spiritual experience (or anyone else's for that matter) on the grounds that he prophesied.

Our conclusions regarding Saul's spiritual status lead to the fact that Saul needed David. Saul's need was obvious when one or two of his worldly escapades required the stern reproof of Samuel, a true prophet of God.

King Saul had to face three enemies: the Philistines, Amalek, and Goliath of Gath. The Philistines represent the *world,* Amalek represents the *flesh,* and Goliath represents the *devil.* Saul fell before each of them. He was unable to deal with his enemies and he needed someone who could. That is why Saul needed David. We need Christ for the same reason.

King Saul represents the kind of person evangelists and soul-winners often meet. This kind of person has an aroused soul, responds somewhat to spiritual things, and even seems to be a Christian, but he really is not saved. He has a questing soul but not a quickened spirit. Many people who come forward during evangelistic services are like that. They make empty professions of faith. They are sincere enough and may even show some of the initial marks of being saved, but they are not truly born again. Some of them go on to their dying day trusting in an experience that fell short of a soul-saving, life-transforming, spirit-regenerating new birth. Soul-winners need to be aware that a "convert" may say the right things and do the right things for a while although a personal love for Christ is lacking. Simon in Acts 8:5-24 is the classic New Testament example.

Saul lacked spiritual life. That became quite evident in his relationship with David. Samuel, great preacher that he was, could awaken Saul's soul to God, but he could never bring Saul into a heart-relationship with either God or David, the Lord's true anointed. There is all the difference in the world between being aroused to a personal need for God and being brought into a personal, quickening relationship with Christ.

Face to face with the Philistines, Amalek, and Goliath, Saul should have known at once that he had no power to deal with his enemies. He should have realized he needed David.

II. HOW DISDAINFULLY HE RIDICULED DAVID

The next step in King Saul's disastrous spiritual odyssey came when he encountered David face to face. What the king did with David, the Lord's true anointed, revealed the shallow nature of Saul's previous religious experiences.

It was during the episode with Goliath that the king reacted to David. Saul was afraid of the one and not willing to accept the other. Every day the giant of Gath scorned and ridiculed the Israelites and their God. King Saul was tall, but he was no match for Goliath. Size and reputation mean nothing to the devil. He is not the least bit afraid of any of us.

When the very thought of going down into the valley of Elah alone to fight Goliath froze Saul's blood, David came. He came in his shepherd character to be Israel's savior.

Saul already knew David. One of Saul's servants had given him a magnificent description: "Behold, I have seen a son of Jesse the Bethlehemite, that is cunning in playing [a testimony to his *competence*], and a mighty valiant man [a testimony to his *courage*], and a man of war [a testimony to his *conquests*], and prudent in matters [a testimony to his *caution*], and a comely person [a testimony to his *charisma*], and the Lord is with him [a testimony to his *character*]" (1 Samuel 16:18). So Saul sent for David, but at that time saw none of the traits so obvious to the servant. Or, if Saul saw them, he resisted them.

Now Saul was face to face with David's sublime trust in God, his superlative courage and conviction, and his total confidence that God would go with him down into the valley. Now Saul had to accept David as savior or else sow the seeds of his own doom. At this critical moment of decision, Saul's reaction to David was a matter of salvation or defeat. What did Saul do? He scoffed at David.

"You!" we can hear Saul exclaim. "You my savior? Nonsense! You are only a boy. Why, I'm three times the man you are. Goliath would make mincemeat of you." Saul had no use for David. In fact Saul would rather have no savior at all than have to acknowledge a debt of salvation to David.

There was no escaping David, however, so Saul would only accept David on Saul's terms. "If this is a matter of salvation," he said in effect, "then I must share in it. I must at least be allowed to contribute to my own salvation. You will have to fight Goliath in my armor."

David, out of courtesy to Saul, put on the armor and then took it all off again. Saul could receive no personal salvation as long as he insisted on making his own contribution to God's plan of salvation. David would not fight Goliath in Saul's armor. It was incongruous. Likewise, if we are to be saved, we must set aside all confidence in our righteousness, our efforts, our ironclad respectability. Our own armor may fit us, but the Lord will have nothing to do with it. We must stop insisting that Christ be our Savior on our terms.

After ridiculing David, Saul rejected David's claim to be the one and only savior. "Thou art but a youth" (1 Samuel 17:33), he sneered, making the common mistake of judging by outward appearance. Israel had chosen Saul to be king in the first place. They had judged him by his outward appearance. Now Saul rejected David as savior on the same carnal grounds. That is why millions reject Christ. Julian the Apostate called Jesus "the pale Galilean." The Nazis called Him "a crucified, dead Jew." Millions think of Him only as "gentle Jesus, meek and mild," and underestimate Him. However, He is God over all, blessed for evermore.

Saul was reluctant to face one obvious fact about David. David was the only savior God had provided for Israel, just as Christ is the only Savior God has provided for us. There was no salvation anywhere else for Saul, and there is "none other name under heaven given among men, whereby we must be saved" (Acts 4:12).

Rejecting Saul's armor and retaining his shepherd character, David turned his back on Saul and set his face toward the valley. He came to grips with Goliath—"him that had the power of death" (Hebrews 2:14)—and destroyed him. Nobody else could have done that. Not Saul, not Jonathan, not Abner nor Joab nor all the host of Israel could have done that. David, and only David, was God's anointed savior that day.

Having conquered Goliath, David returned victorious from the fight. Across the country, from Dan to Beersheba, from Manasseh to the Mediterranean, from north to south, from east to west, from busy city markets to rural hamlets in the hills, the great shout went up: "Saul hath slain his thousands, *and David his ten thousands"* (1 Samuel 18:7, italics added). The Israelites thought of David and declared, in effect, "Hallelujah! What a savior!" But Saul had no intention of bowing his knee to David or of heralding his praise.

III. HOW DEEPLY HE RESENTED DAVID

Jealousy, rage, and resentment—black as the pit of Hell and as cruel as the grave—entered Saul's soul. He hated David from that day on. Moreover he hated all who dared to make it known that they had accepted David as savior and anticipated his return as sovereign.

Saul's hatred came home to roost in his own home. Both Jonathan and Michal gave their hearts to David. Attempting to change Jonathan's mind, Saul tried persuasion first. He cursed Jonathan and his mother. "Use your head, man," we can hear Saul say. "Can't you see that David will ruin your career? I've never heard anything so senseless in my life. Why throw away all your prospects for the sake of David?"

When Saul found that persuasion was getting him nowhere, he tried outright persecution. He flung a javelin at his son (1 Samuel 20:33). Jonathan, however, possessed a temper equal to Saul's, and Saul never tried that tactic again. But Saul was able to put sufficient pressure on his son to force him to settle for a life of compromise (Jonathan never followed the leading of his heart to go with David). Saul thus robbed Jonathan of his crown at the second coming of David—that is, when David typically returned to come into his kingdom.

To sway Michal, Saul resorted to cunning. He said in effect, "If you're determined to give your heart to David, I can't prevent that. Go ahead and marry him. Just remember, you might be David's wife, but you're still my daughter. You'll do what I tell you or it will be the worse for you." And thus it was. Michal lived such a life of compromise that she brought dishonor on David's name.

Saul resented David and everything David stood for. Saul resented David because he was both savior and sovereign and because he was the Lord's anointed. Saul resented David because his godly life showed up Saul's glaring sins. Saul resented David for his knowledge of God and his popular psalms. Saul hated the thought that people all over the land were singing David's songs and singing his praise. Saul resented David because he avoided the snares that were set for his feet. Saul resented David for not using the same carnal weapons that were used against him. Saul resented David's goodness, his grace, his gifts, his greatness, and his coming glory. Saul resented David because he was always beyond reach. Saul resented David because in the end the kingdom, the power, and the glory would all be his. Saul resented David because he had provided salvation in the dark valley of death and there could have been no salvation without him.

In other words, Saul resented David for the same reasons that people today resent and reject Christ.

IV. HOW DELIBERATELY HE REJECTED DAVID

Saul's life degenerated into a mad crusade against David. He summoned all the allies he could find. He gathered around him men who hated David, and made short work of anyone suspected of siding with David.

The terrible incident in 1 Samuel 22 is an example. Saul finally and fully revealed what a murderous heart he had. When David went to Gath, he stopped near Jerusalem at Nob, the place where the tabernacle was pitched, and appealed to Ahimelech the priest for bread. Ahimelech reluctantly gave David the sacred shewbread from the table of the tabernacle and Goliath's sword, which was kept in the tabernacle compound as a national treasure.

One of Saul's cronies, an evil man named Doeg the Edomite, took great delight in informing Saul of Ahimelech's "disloyalty." That was enough for Saul. He ordered the massacre of the entire priestly family residing at Nob. Eighty-five priests were among the victims in that holocaust. The murder of God's anointed priests was on Saul's conscience until the end of his days. The crime with its attendant guilt was a direct result of Saul's rejection of David.

It is hard for us to realize that some people today hate Christ as much as Saul hated David. They hate Christ and they hate His people. There is no end to the harm these hateful people will try to inflict on believers.

V. HOW DREADFULLY HE REPUDIATED DAVID

David spared Saul's life on two separate occasions. David never stopped loving poor, deluded, demented, demon-driven Saul. David would have saved him, even at the very end, if Saul had let him. David never desired the death of Saul. Some of David's own people never could understand why David did not kill Saul when the opportunity arose. But David, like Jesus, loved even his enemies.

On one of the occasions when David could have slain the king, Saul confessed, "I have played the fool" (1 Samuel 26:21). But he continued to play that role. A man like Saul plays the fool once too often. Saul's bitterness toward David was noted in Heaven. In the end God allowed the Philistines to invade the land. Saul knew that the only man in the kingdom who could deal with the Philistines was David, but even in this emergency he would not call on David to be his savior.

Saul called upon God, but God no longer spoke to him. Saul had sinned away the day of grace. Samuel the prophet was dead and with his death the last restraining influence had passed out of Saul's life. The silence of God in all its abysmal horror descended on Saul's soul. Terrible indeed is the condition of the person to whom God no longer speaks, at the door of whose heart God no longer knocks.

In his desperate need, Saul had only two places to go. He could go to David, plead with him for forgiveness, and in deep contrition hand over the affairs of the kingdom. But Saul would rather die than take such a humble place. Instead of going to David, Saul went to a witch. He turned to the occult. He went down to Endor and pleaded with the witch who lived there to summon up Samuel from the dead.

A great deal of hocus-pocus is circulated about spiritism and astrology, but there is also reality in the whole devilish field. There is a reality behind the occult and it is an evil reality. Those who play with ouija boards or attend seances are opening the doors of their personalities to an occult invasion. Behind the occult lurks the evil one and a vast army of deceiving spirits.

The Bible expressly forbids any communication with a witch (today we would call the person a psychic). The spiritual consequences of such communication are so terrible that God ordered the death penalty for those who practice witchcraft. In defiance of the Word of God King Saul consulted the witch.

The usual practice was for the witch to contact her familiar spirit, who would impersonate the spirit the client wished to contact—or her familiar spirit could have one of his demon colleagues do the impersonation. This time, to the horror and fright of the witch, the impossible happened. Samuel himself appeared. And Samuel pronounced the death sentence on Saul.

Finding the door of Heaven barred against him, this desperate man deliberately repudiated David and knocked on the door of Hell. God opened the door for Saul—and let him fall through it. Within a day he was dead and damned.

A person can ridicule, resent, and repudiate the claims of Christ, and God will let him do it. God will sometimes stay His hand twenty, thirty, forty, or fifty years. Then all of a sudden the sentence will fall. The summons into eternity will come. The Christ-rejecter will be dead and in Hell. That is the lesson of Saul.

4
Lot,
the Saddest Reminder

Genesis 13:11; 14; 19:12; Luke 17:32

The only way a man is ever counted righteous by God is by *believing*. The Bible says, "Abraham believed God, and it was counted unto him for righteousness" (Romans 4:3). Somewhere along the line Lot too put his faith and trust in the

Lord and was accounted righteous in Heaven's sight. Indeed
God calls him "that righteous man" (2 Peter 2:8). That is, He
puts Lot on a par with Abraham, one of the greatest believers
of all time. But we would never guess from what is revealed
about Lot in Genesis that he was a believer. Were it not for the
fact that the Holy Spirit notes that Lot was righteous, we would
probably write him off as one who merely professed to believe.

An old English proverb says, "You can't have both the
penny and the bun." Lot wanted both. He wanted the best of
both worlds. That is the mistake Lot made.

All people have to ask themselves two questions. The first
is, Heaven or Hell? Once we settle that question and strike out
for Heaven, the second question follows quickly: Heaven or
earth? The devil tries to persuade believers that the second
question doesn't matter—that as long as their souls are saved,
they can try to get everything this world offers. When we look
at Lot, however, we see the enormous cost of choosing to live
for worldly gain. In this chapter we will trace the downward
course of this man who once made a decision for God that
ensured his name would be written in life's eternal book, yet
failed to make his calling and election sure.

The world is the sworn enemy of God, and God is the
sworn enemy of the world. "If any man love the world, the love
of the Father is not in him" (1 John 2:15). "The world," of
course, is human life and society with God left out. God has
never blessed worldliness, and He never will. The life of Lot is
an example of worldliness. His story is told in Genesis to warn
others not to make the same mistake he made; he is held up
as a lighthouse to help others avoid shipwreck.

I. LOT'S CHOICE

Lot had come under the godly influence of his Uncle
Abraham. Swept off his feet by Abraham's dynamic faith, his
all-out commitment to God, and his determination to walk the
straight and narrow way, Lot too had struck out on the pilgrim

way. The two men had traveled a long way together. They had journeyed north from Ur and then west across the fertile crescent. They had continued on past the great city of Damascus and gone down into Canaan. God had led each step of the way and had blessed not only Abraham but Lot as well. "And Abram," we read, "was very rich in cattle, in silver, and in gold. . . . And Lot also, which went with Abram, had flocks, and herds, and tents" (Genesis 13:2,5).

So far so good. But then a dispute arose.

A. The Dispute

"And there was a strife between the herdmen of Abram's cattle and the herdmen of Lot's cattle: and the Canaanite and the Perizzite dwelled then in the land" (Genesis 13:7). The devil had won a victory. Here were two believers in the midst of a crooked and perverse generation, and their testimony for God was being destroyed.

Genesis 13 is the first chapter in the Bible where the word *brethren* appears—and there they were quarreling. At least their servants and supporters were. They squabbled over money, over material things, over what Paul contemptuously called "filthy lucre" (1 Timothy 3:3). Satan had these two households occupied with the things of this world. Having taken their eyes off the Lord and eternal things, they disagreed over who had grazing rights to the limited pastureland.

B. The Discussion

So Abraham and Lot had a discussion. God had deeded the whole land to Abraham. It was all his. However, he turned to Lot and said in effect: "Look here, Lot. We are brethren. The things that divide us are nothing compared with the things that unite us. Here we are squabbling over a few thousand acres of land. Let us keep eternity's values in view. Take your choice, my brother. I'll leave the matter in God's hands. It is far better that we should separate than that we should squabble— especially in front of the ungodly."

A spiritual man—a man who has learned to leave circumstances with God—speaks from a perspective like Abraham's.

C. The Decision

Lot made his choice, and we note what he decided and why. He had a terrible lack in his life. He had no spiritual priorities, no spiritual perspective. He was *weak in his devotions*. We read that Abraham had an altar and that he "called on the name of the Lord" (Genesis 13:4). We do not read that of Lot. He somehow managed to jog along from day to day without any personal quiet time with God. No wonder his life was a spiritual shipwreck. None of us can live the Christian life unless we daily cast our anchor, haul in our sails, and get alone with the Lord. We will drift if we do not do that, and the reefs are waiting for us.

Lot was also *worldly in his desires*. Lot chose the well-watered plain of Jordan because it reminded him of Egypt. In Old Testament typology, Egypt is one of the symbols of the world. Lot was Heaven-born and Heaven-bound, but he had the world in his heart. When Abraham first suggested that they separate, Lot should have become alarmed. He should have said: "What? Leave the fellowship of God's people? Neglect the assembly of the saints? Try to 'go it alone' surrounded by Canaanites and Perizzites? God forbid! The price is too high." Instead Lot made a carnal worldly choice. He had a *"religious"* reason for his choice: the coveted spot was "even as the garden of the Lord." His *"real"* reason was that the plain of Jordan was "like the land of Egypt" (Genesis 13:10).

Lot was *wrong in his decisions*. He thought he was a much stronger believer than he really was. He thought he could live independently of Abraham and his household of like-minded men. Lot thought he could start his own group in Sodom. The Holy Spirit adds this significant comment on Lot's choice: "But the men of Sodom were wicked and sinners before the Lord exceedingly" (Genesis 13:13). God had already marked Sodom for judgment. It was the last place on earth that

Lot should have chosen. But he had no spiritual anchor and no spiritual awareness, so he drifted toward Sodom, blissfully ignorant of the caldrons of fire and brimstone already bubbling and boiling on high. Some might object that Lot did not know that Sodom was doomed. But God knew, and had Lot taken time to wait on God, God would have directed his steps elsewhere.

II. LOT'S CHAINS

Lot moved his family into Sodom. His children grew up with Sodomites instead of with saints. His wife went shopping in Sodom when she should have stayed with Sarah.

Any person who moves out of the will of God will face the consequences sooner or later. Lot was no exception. War broke out and Sodom was defeated. Lot, his wife, and his little ones were caught up in the maelstrom and swept away with the tide. The victorious kings of the East fastened chains on the hands of Lot and his family and marched them away with the ungodly to be sold in the slave markets of Mesopotamia. Lot had chosen the world so God let him have the world—and its chains.

What did Lot think about as he trudged along with a yoke of iron around his neck and a whip cracking over his head? What did he think when he saw one of his little ones stumble and then scream with pain as the slave driver thrashed him and kicked him back into line? What did Lot think when he saw a soldier leering at his wife or overheard one of them telling his friends how much he thought she was worth? What did he think as he marched north and saw the smoke of Abraham's campfires on the hill?

Lot's chains were the direct result of Lot's choice. Let us not deceive ourselves. If we deliberately allow the world to come between us and the Lord and His people, we will pay for it. Our circumstances will close in on us in the end. There will be little hope for us either, unless some Christian brother cares for us the way Abraham cared for Lot. Lot had treated Abraham badly, but that "friend of God" held no grudges. When he heard the news of Lot's chains, Abraham mobilized his forces and called on his brethren for help. Then away he went, at great personal cost and risk, to rescue his nephew. Abraham rescued not only Lot, but also all those who were with him. Genesis 14 records the resounding victory.

Abraham, the man God used to rescue Lot, knew the meaning of true separation. Separation is not isolation, but insulation. The truly separated believer is like a live electrical wire—insulated against that which would cause a short circuit, and in touch with the need at one end and the power at the other. God can use such a man in an hour of crisis.

Lot was rescued. His chains were removed. He could have started all over again. He could have come back into the fellowship of God's people. He could have brought up his family in a spiritual atmosphere instead of in a Sodomite environment. He could have said to his uncle: "Dear Abraham, I was wrong. I am sorry for my selfishness. Will you receive me back into fellowship?" But that was not what Lot did.

III. LOT'S CHANCE

Abraham sat at the Lord's table with Melchizedek. With the bread and wine before him, Abraham poured out his heartfelt thanks in a tangible offering of his tithes. And where was Lot? Absent from the service and in a conference of quite a different kind.

Abraham and Melchizedek were fellowshiping over the emblems of the Lord's body and blood. That was the scene in the camp of Abraham—the separated, victorious believer.

Meanwhile Lot was with the rejoicing, liberated captives. He was talking and laughing with the Sodomites, who were congratulating him for having connections with so mighty a military leader as Abraham.

The king of Sodom was probably talking with the king of

Gomorrah and laughing over some vile joke when Lot came into view. We can almost see the king of Sodom stroke his beard reflectively and say to the king of Gomorrah: "I say, Birsha, we should keep in with that fellow Lot. If his uncle is such a warrior, we need to keep on his good side. I have already tried the old boy out—you know, offered him a king's ransom—but the old fool has religious mania. He refuses any kind of connection with us at all. But there is no denying he knows how to fight. If we can't tie Abraham to our apron strings, we had better tie his nephew Lot to us."

So the king of Sodom summoned Lot. Lot came and bowed respectfully. "Lot," we can hear the king say, "I have taken a great liking to you, my son. You are just the kind of man Sodom needs. We need you in the government. Would you be interested in a well-paying, influential position at court? What do you say to being made a minister of state in Sodom?"

Lot thought that this offer was his big chance. The poor foolish man had not learned a thing. Abraham's efforts to rescue him from his backsliding had all been in vain.

We can trace the progression of worldliness in Lot's life. First he *looked* toward Sodom; then he *pitched his tent* toward Sodom; then he *dwelled* in Sodom. The next time we meet him he is *sitting in the gate* of Sodom, the place of government in cities of old.

IV. LOT'S CHILDREN

The Holy Spirit gives us one more look at Lot on the night of Sodom's judgment. The hot fires of God's wrath against the sexual sins of Sodom had been banked up for years, but grace had held back His hand. That night, however, judgment was to fall.

Two angels of God inspected the city and found the reports of Sodom's unnatural sins to be true beyond all doubt. Those vices did not slink down the back alleys, furtive and ashamed. They stalked brazenly on the major thoroughfares.

The gay community demanded its rights. Society acknowledged the perverted preferences of the gays to be normal and permissible. Their alternative lifestyle was upheld by the laws of the land. The streets of Sodom were utterly vile. Visitors were not safe in Sodom, not even in the home of a minister of state. Judgment must fall, so Lot was sent running through the city to warn his children.

Lot had never asked if Sodom was a good place to raise children. He just asked if the plain of Jordan was a good place to raise cattle. Lot had never worried much about the spiritual welfare of his children. He had thought his example would be sufficient. After all, he had never indulged in those gross sins for which Sodom was famous. He had doubtless told his children about Abraham and God, but he had never wept and prayed for their salvation. He had never cared enough for his children to separate himself from Sodom.

Lot had sent his children to Sodom's schools and he had allowed them to play with Sodom's sons. He had watched his children imbibe Sodom's values and accept Sodom's vices. He had allowed his wife to become more and more involved in the social life of Sodom. Then he had wondered why his family was slipping away from him.

At least two of his daughters had married into Sodomite families. He had lost them! They cared nothing at all for spiritual things. Payday had arrived. He had sowed worldliness, and he had reaped worldliness. He had "vexed his righteous soul from day to day," the New Testament says (2 Peter 2:8), but little good that could do as long as he continued to live in Sodom. Why couldn't he see that? Why didn't he get right with God? Why don't we?

Sometimes we see our children absorbing the world's values. They argue over every little thing. They don't want anything to do with the Lord's people; they prefer their godless friends. And we wonder why. But if we have modeled a lifestyle of worldliness, no wonder our children are like that. Does the hymn writer describe our lifestyle?

> Room for pleasure, room for business—
> But, for Christ the Crucified,
> Not a place where He can enter
> In the heart for which He died?

Like so many people today, Lot had a saved soul and a lost life. He made the world his choice and then wondered why his children did not have the slightest interest in spiritual things. Lot pursued worldly goals and had to reap worldly results.

The Bible gives us two dreadful closing glimpses of Lot's children. They had fully absorbed the viewpoint and vices of Sodom.

A. They Had the Viewpoint of Sodom

Look first at his married daughters and their husbands. When Lot hammered on their doors that night of judgment, they rolled over, then turned out of bed to see what on earth was the matter. "Hurry!" we can almost hear Lot say. "Judgment day has come! God is going to destroy Sodom. Two angels have visited me. They have seen for themselves the sins of Sodom and they are going to pour out God's wrath on this place. Hurry! Don't even get dressed. Just seize a cloak and come. They will save us if we hurry."

It was God's solemn, sober truth. "But he seemed as one that mocked unto his sons in law" (Genesis 19:14). His daughters had the viewpoint of Sodom too. They did not believe a word Lot was saying. What else could he have expected? His testimony was not backed up by the kind of life that would have made his words credible. Many a parent has awakened too late to that sad fact.

B. They Had the Vices of Sodom

Now look at the two daughters who still lived at home. The angels dragged them out of the city and the two girls fled for the hills. Their mother was dead—turned into a pillar of salt because she looked back lovingly and longingly at Sodom. The two unwed daughters were now alone in the hills with their father. What they did to him is recorded in Genesis 19. They committed incest. The angels had been able to get the girls out of Sodom, but the angels had not been able to get Sodom out of the girls.

So much for Lot's children. But what about our own? What kind of example are we setting day by day? What are our priorities? What principles guide us in the decisions we make? Our children know.

There is still time to change our ways, but the longer we delay, the more difficult and costly the change will be. We must repent. We must get back into full, participating fellowship with the Lord's people. We must put God first in everything. We must fast and pray and take time to be holy. We must safeguard our daily quiet time as the most important, precious, and vital activity in our lives. We must allow God to transform our lives. We must besiege His throne and hammer at Heaven's door like that importunate woman in the Gospels. We must say to God, as Jacob did, "I will not let thee go, except thou bless me" (Genesis 32:26). We must be importunate with God to save and sanctify our children while we put their feet on the road that leads to eternal life.

Then God will go to work for us. He is waiting to step into our hopeless situations and work spiritual miracles *for* us. But first He has to work spiritual miracles *in* us.

I have often thought what a pity it was that Lot did not take his two unmarried daughters to Hebron, so that at least these two might come under the influence of godly Abraham. Who knows what might have happened then?

5
Stephen,
the First Martyr

Acts 6:1–7:60

I. THE FAITHFUL MINISTER
II. THE FEARLESS MESSENGER
III. THE FIRST MARTYR

The deacons of the early church were excellent men. Two of them, Stephen and Philip, leaped almost immediately to high prominence, outshining even the apostles.

Stephen became the first great *martyr* of the church. He was the vanguard of the army of faithful Christians who through the centuries would die boldly for the cause of Christ. Nero would sew Christians up in blood-soaked sacks and throw them to wild beasts. He would dip believers in tar and use them as living torches for his revels. Torquemada would torture Christians to death during the Inquisition. They would be burned at the stake and massacred by the thousands. Leading the way was Stephen, one of the deacons.

Stephen's friend Philip became the first *missionary* of the church. He took seriously the words of the Lord Jesus: "Ye shall be witnesses unto me . . . in Samaria" (Acts 1:8). None of the apostles wanted to go to Samaria, although James and John had once been willing enough to call down fire on Samaria (Luke 9:54). So the deacon Philip went to Samaria first. Soon revival broke out there. The ranks of the Jewish church were breached and it was forced to take its first mighty step toward becoming an international community of called-out ones. Leading the way "into all the world" was Philip, one of the deacons.

The early church would not appoint anyone to be a deacon unless he was filled with the Spirit. Stephen was just such a man.

I. THE FAITHFUL MINISTER

The early church was expanding rapidly. Thousands were being saved and added to its ranks, and the apostles were very busy. Extraordinary things were happening. There was a great outpouring of love in the church and the Christians were generously giving money to fund their social welfare program. Then the devil saw an opportunity. (Christians probably squabble over money more than anything else.) Some of the widows began to complain that they were not getting their fair share. A stream of people with petty complaints soon distracted the apostles. We can imagine the grievances. "Mrs. Smith was given four dollars more than I was and I have two more children than she has." "Mrs. Jones got beef and I only got chicken." "Mrs. Murphy was given a wool blanket and I only received a cotton one."

Peter, who was a practical businessman, decided that enough was enough. It was time to delegate the secular and social side of the ministry to other men. But not just anybody! Perhaps anyone could wait on tables in a secular soup kitchen, but only those with the highest qualifications should wait on tables in the church. The apostles did not say, "Find someone who has proved himself successful in handling money." They did not say, "Find someone who has a degree in business management." The qualifications for a deacon were much more stringent than that. The apostles said, "Look ye out among you seven men of honest report, full of the Holy Ghost and wisdom, whom we may appoint over this business" (Acts 6:3). Manward the deacons had to be "men of honest report." Godward they had to be "full of the Holy Ghost." Selfward they had to be "full of . . . wisdom."

In other words, deacons had to be men of *sterling character*. Their integrity had to be beyond question. They had to be people who could be trusted, people who had unstained reputations. They not only had to *be* honest; everybody had to *know* they were honest.

Deacons also had to be men of *spiritual capacity*. In the early church nothing less than a complete filling of the Holy Spirit would suffice—even to do the most humble, menial task.

Finally deacons had to be men of *simple competence*. They had to be full of wisdom. They had to be able to make sensible decisions. (Unfortunately, spirituality and common sense are often strangers to one another.)

Stephen met the qualifications. He was honest, capable, and Spirit-filled—that is, the loveliness of the Lord Jesus characterized everything he did. A person who is filled with the Spirit is intoxicated with the Holy Spirit. He is turned into a different kind of person. He becomes Christlike in his walk and in his talk. He experiences the present, continuous process referred to in Ephesians 5:18: literally, "Be ye being filled."

The Holy Spirit says this about a deacon: "They that have used the office of a deacon well purchase to themselves a good degree, and great boldness in the faith which is in Christ Jesus" (1 Timothy 3:13). In other words, the office of a deacon is one of God's schools for the development of spirituality, character, and talent.

Stephen certainly developed boldness in the faith. He made full proof of his ministry. He was "full of faith and power, [and] did great wonders and miracles among the people" (Acts 6:8). What those miracles were is of little or no importance today. What is important is that Stephen manifested the power of God in his life. He made an impact for God on his generation. He waited on tables, as Dr. Luke put it (Acts 6:2). He ministered in ever-widening circles to the physical and spiritual needs of his flock.

Stephen was not famous just for his mighty works. He soon developed into an effective preacher of the gospel. We read: "Then there arose certain of the . . . Libertines, and Cyrenians, and Alexandrians, and of them of Cilicia and of Asia, disputing with Stephen. And they were not able to resist the wisdom and the spirit by which he spake" (Acts 6:9-10). These hot debates probably took place in the Jerusalem synagogue frequented by Hellenist Jews.

The mention of Cilicia points us to the Roman province of Asia Minor and to its capital city of Tarsus. The strong inference is that the brilliant young Jew, Saul of Tarsus, was a member of the synagogue where the debates took place. Saul was a trained rabbi, a disciple of the famous Gamaliel, and a formidable opponent in debate. He was a dedicated Jew, a convinced Talmudist, and a bigoted Pharisee. He was convinced that Jesus of Nazareth was an apostate and that Christianity was a blasphemous and dangerous cult. Saul had a mind for the universe—narrowed by rabbinic Judaism. He had a mind capable of writing such world-shaking Epistles as Romans, Ephesians, and Thessalonians, but his horizons were limited by the traditions and teachings of men like Hillel and Gamaliel.

We can well imagine that Saul and Stephen frequently locked horns over the issue of Jesus of Nazareth. Stephen would calmly point to the Old Testament Scriptures and say: "There were not to be two *Christs*—one to suffer and one to reign. There were to be two *comings.*

"Look at the evidence of the life that Jesus lived, Saul. Jesus was not a blasphemer. He was the Son of God. He walked on the waves and stilled the storm. He turned water into wine and fed hungry multitudes. He healed the sick and cleansed lepers. He cast out evil spirits and raised the dead. It is impossible to deny the life that He lived. And as for His death— that was redemptive. He died, the just for us the unjust, to bring us to God.

"He fulfilled the law and the words of the prophets. He fulfilled such Scriptures as Isaiah 53, Psalm 22, and Psalm 69. The Scriptures say that His hands and feet were to be pierced. The prophet said He was to be numbered with the transgressors.

"Then to crown it all He rose from the dead. Come, come, Saul! The Sanhedrin says that the disciples stole the body, but you are an intelligent man. You know that can't be true. Why didn't the Sanhedrin arrest Peter and John and the rest and put them on trial? Why didn't Caiaphas make them show where the body was hidden? You know as well as I do, Saul, that they did not dare to do any such thing. There was no body to produce. I can introduce you to more than five hundred people who saw Jesus alive after His resurrection. You can cross-examine them if you like. All Jerusalem knows He rose from the dead. This thing was not done in a corner . . . "

Stephen taught the Scriptures with authority. And so the debate went on until Saul and his friends gnashed their teeth in rage.

II. THE FEARLESS MESSENGER

"If you can't persuade them, persecute them!" Before long the Jewish leaders arrested Stephen, put him on trial, and indicted him on two counts. They accused him of attacking the *Scriptures* and the *sanctuary*. His spoken defense is a masterpiece, one of the truly great sermons in the book of Acts. Stephen's defense ranks alongside Peter's Pentecostal sermon, Paul's sermon in Pisidian Antioch, and Paul's message on Mars Hill.

Throughout the ages the church has produced magnificent preachers and powerful sermons. We think of Jonathan

Edwards and his "Sinners in the Hands of an Angry God" and of Henry Drummond and his "The Greatest Thing in the World." We think of Spurgeon and D. L. Moody, men who could move the masses with their words. Stephen stands in the forefront of them all.

Stephen's defense revolved around three major points. He talked to his enemies about the saviors, the Scriptures, and the sanctuaries God had given them.

God had given them *saviors* like Joseph and Moses, but Israel had rejected them. False witnesses were accusing Stephen of speaking against Moses when Israel's whole national history had been characterized by setting Moses aside. Stephen's accusers were far more guilty than he was.

God had given Israel the *Scriptures,* but they had broken the law. The nation had plunged into the grossest idolatry despite what the Scriptures said about such folly. Now the Jewish leaders were trying to restructure the law by imposing all their vain traditions on it. Stephen's accusers were the ones who were guilty of speaking against the Scriptures.

God had given Israel *sanctuaries:* first a tabernacle and then a temple. The temple was David's idea, not God's, although God accepted David's generous thought. Solomon built the temple, but had enough sense to see that his sanctuary—lavish and magnificent though it was—could not house a God who inhabited all the vast reaches of time and space. In Stephen's day his enemies called their temple a holy place, but all they had done was defile it.

The tabernacle was different. It spoke of the transient and temporary, for God never stands still. God cannot be locked up in a temple, though it be made of gold, silver, precious stones, costly wood, and rich fabrics, and though it be served with expensive offerings and rare perfumes.

"The very idea! To think that the great, eternal, uncreated, self-existent God of the universe, the Creator of stars and worlds unknown, could be shut up in a tiny temple on an obscure hill by a stiff-necked and rebellious crowd of religious fanatics . . . " Stripped down to its bare essentials, that was what Stephen told his accusers, the religious elite of the nation. It made them mad!

But Stephen was not through speaking. Amid a growing uproar of fury and dissent, he hammered home his conclusion. They had accused him of *reviling the holy place*. He accused them of *resisting the Holy Ghost*. They had accused him of *slighting Moses, the man of God*. He accused them of *slaying Jesus, the Son of God*. They had accused him of *blaspheming the law*. He accused them of *breaking the law*. Stephen took the charges leveled against him, picked them up, and flung them back in the faces of his accusers. We read, "When they heard these things, they were cut to the heart, and they gnashed on him with their teeth" (Acts 7:54). (Doubtless Luke heard of what happened at this trial from Paul, who was among that mob of angry men.) They were turned into a pack of wolves. Everywhere Stephen looked he saw faces distorted with fury and rage.

III. THE FIRST MARTYR

Having hammered home God's truth, noble Stephen looked away from that ring of furious faces. He looked up. Luke wrote, "He, being full of the Holy Ghost, looked up stedfastly into heaven, and saw the glory of God [that is, the Shekinah glory cloud, long missing from the earthly temple], and Jesus standing on the right hand of God" (Acts 7:55). And Stephen instantly bore witness to what he saw.

Just two short years before, Jesus had returned to Heaven, having been absent from His homeland for more than thirty-three years. He had come from glory to visit a distant planet in the remote galaxy that men would one day call the Milky Way. He had returned home in a battle-scarred human body, but He had been given a triumphal entry into Heaven. He had assumed once more the glory He had with the Father before the worlds began. We can almost picture His welcome. The gates of glory had swung wide. The trumpets had blared. The angel choirs, massed along the streets of gold leading to the great white throne, had sung the Hallelujah Chorus until it echoed off the everlasting hills. Angels and archangels, thrones and dominions, cherubim and seraphim, had joined the grand procession. Cheering, chanting, and applauding, the mighty throng had paraded up to Zion's hill. All Heaven had rung with the praise of the shining ones: "Holy! Holy! Holy is the Lord!" The twenty-four elders had cast their crowns at His feet, and He had sat down at the right hand of the Majesty on high.

That is where Jesus was when Stephen saw Him. No less than sixteen times in the Bible Jesus is said to be at God's right hand. No less than thirteen times Jesus is said to be seated at the right hand of God. The word *seated* shows that the work of salvation has been completed to the eternal satisfaction of God. The word *seated* shows that though He is man, Jesus is also God. He is God the Son—coequal, coeternal, and coexistent with the Father—God over all, blessed for evermore. Jesus is seated, "henceforth expecting till his enemies be made his footstool" (Hebrews 10:13).

The day Stephen was tried admiring angels still crowded around Jesus. They gazed on the face of incarnate deity. They looked in awe and wonder at the marks of Calvary. Their eyes were riveted on Him, but He was not looking at them. He was looking back to earth where He saw Stephen standing alone surrounded by a howling mob of scribes and Sadducees, rulers and rabbis, priests and Pharisees. Their faces were distorted with rage, their lips drawn back from gnashing teeth. Hatred was in their eyes and death was in their hands. There Stephen stood—one lone man, careless of his life, a latecomer to the ministry—bravely telling the mob the truth about Jesus. This is the scene Jesus saw and it was all too familiar.

The slow fuse Stephen had lighted with his very first word had reached the powder keg. It exploded with fury and violence. The mob seized him and dragged him from the chamber into the blazing sunshine. They marched him through the city streets, dragged him to the foot of a skull-shaped hill, and prepared for the assault.

Saul of Tarsus cheered the mob on. "Here, you fellows, let me hold your coats," he said. The stones began to fly. And with every stone the mob threw at Stephen they were guaranteeing for themselves a full measure of God's righteous wrath. Was it stones they were looking for? He would give them stones. Within a few decades or so He would tear down their precious temple stone by stone. He would summon the Romans to bring their catapults and engines of war and throw stones at the Jews. First they had rejected the Savior and nailed Him to a cross of wood. Now they had rejected the Holy Spirit and were murdering a blood-bought, Spirit-baptized, Spirit-indwelt, Spirit-sealed, Spirit-filled, and Spirit-anointed child of God.

Luke wrote: "They stoned Stephen, calling upon God, and saying, Lord Jesus, receive my spirit. And he kneeled down, and cried with a loud voice, Lord, lay not this sin to their charge. And when he had said this, he fell asleep" (Acts 7:59-60).

Saul was also destined to wear a martyr's crown, although nothing could have been further from his thoughts the day he witnessed Stephen's death. That day iron entered into Saul's soul. Whether it was Stephen's face, or his message, or his calm assurance, or his forgiveness, or his testimony that he had seen the standing Christ, something affected Saul that day. Saul would never forget Stephen. That angel face (Acts 6:15) would haunt him until the face of Stephen was replaced in his soul by the face of Jesus, the Son of God.

When the stoning of Stephen was all over, devout men picked up the battered body of the first Christian martyr. They washed it, wrapped it, and gave it a decent burial. Then they met to decide what to do. It was evident that savage persecution would now be let loose on the church. They had seen the face of Stephen, but they had also seen the face of Saul. They had seen the blood-lust, the hatred, the zeal, the fanaticism, and the determination of that young man.

Doubtless those devout men wept for Stephen too. He had shown such promise. *Why,* they must have wondered, *did God allow this to happen?* Ah, but they could not see Stephen. While they mourned, he was receiving "the stephanus"—the martyr's crown. If they could have seen Stephen at that moment, they would not have wept. They would have laughed for joy. They would have seen angels crowding around him to welcome him home. The mourners would have seen him conducted amid triumphant anthems to where Christ was sitting at God's right hand. They would have seen him bow at Jesus' feet. They would have seen him—the spirit of a just man made perfect—enter into the joy of his reward. They would have heard all Heaven echo with the Lord's "Well Done!" They would have heard Christ say: "Welcome home, Stephen. Now let me tell you about that young man Saul . . . "

6
Anna,
the Godliest Widow

Luke 2:36-38

I. HER VICTORY
   She could have been
   A. Bitter at the Funeral
   B. Bitter over Her Family
   C. Bitter over Her Frailty
   D. Bitter over Her Finances
II. HER VOCATION
III. HER VISION

Anna was a very old woman. She had been a widow for eighty-four years and had been married for seven years before that. That accounts for ninety-one years. Even if she had married when she was a young teenager, she would still be over a hundred years old. Anna was a woman who had grown old loving God with all her heart and all her mind and all her soul and all her strength.

Anna was from the tribe of Asher. Asher, the least important of all the tribes, had sprung from the son of Jacob and Leah's maid Zilpah. Leah was the unwanted wife and Zilpah was the unwanted slave of the unwanted wife. Asher was the last and least of the four slave-born sons of Jacob.

Yet Asher never allowed that status to bother him. His name means "happy." He made up for the deficiency of his birth by the joy and gladness of his disposition. Just because a person comes from humble circumstances doesn't mean he cannot be happy. Anna was born into the "happy tribe" and she seems to have imbibed the two characteristics of that tribe: she was humble and she was happy.

Anna added another characteristic: she was not only humble and happy—she was holy. She had grown old in godliness.

This Anna is the godly old woman whose name is forever associated with the birth of the Lord Jesus Christ. She is the woman whom God allowed to see His Son when He was a tiny infant, a baby six or seven weeks old. She saw a little one who was dependent for every human need upon the ministry of a mother; yet Anna realized He was the One on whom the worlds depended. He was the creator and sustainer of the universe—the One who, even when cradled in this mother's arms, upheld all things by the word of His power.

The Lord Jesus had been circumcised when he was eight days old, probably on the last and greatest day of the feast of tabernacles. After the appropriate lapse of time, Mary had now come to the temple with her holy child to offer the sacrifice demanded by the law to cover her uncleanness. A mother had to bring such a sacrifice forty days after the birth of a son, or eighty days after the birth of a daughter (Leviticus 12:2-5).

On this particular occasion God allowed two people to hold His Son in their arms. One was a woman; one was a man. Both were old. The two who were given a special glimpse of Him at this time were Anna and Simeon. They make an interesting pair, but we are only going to look at what the Holy

Spirit records about Anna. We are going to consider the victory, the vocation, and the vision of this remarkable woman.

I. HER VICTORY

When studying people in the Bible of whom very little is told, we must read between the lines. We must flesh out the stories and put ourselves in the people's shoes. When we read between the lines of Luke 2:36-38, we can at once see that Anna was a woman who had achieved victory over bitterness. She could have been very bitter over her lot in life.

A. Bitter at the Funeral

She was young, she was married, and she was happy. She was probably in her late teens or early twenties when the tragedy happened: her husband died and she was left a widow.

Anna could have been very bitter at her husband's funeral. We all know people who have turned bitter after a bereavement. They blame God for their sorrow; they speak rashly and accuse Him of cruelty. Satan wins a victory by distorting their picture of God. But death is not God's fault; death is our fault. The wages of sin is death. We have no one but ourselves to thank for the fact that death stalks the earth invading every home, breaking up every marriage, and turning this world into one vast graveyard. The blame for this blight can all be laid at the door of sin.

Anna might easily have blamed God. She could have decided to turn against Him; millions do. But had she become bitter, in time she would have turned into a sour old woman nobody liked.

With her husband dead, Anna probably had to work to make ends meet. At harvest time she would glean in the fields, doing hard labor for the equivalent of a minimal wage just to survive the winter. She would come home at night and see her husband's work shoes in the corner of the room and his old robe hanging in the closet. The house would be empty and silent but full of haunting memories. Her life was so very, very dark.

But then Anna would take down the family Bible, find a well-worn passage in the prophecy of Isaiah, and read there of "the *treasures* of darkness" (Isaiah 45:3, italics added). Anna learned to trust God in the dark. She would say, "Dear Lord, I don't know why You took my beloved from me, but I trust You anyway. You have promised to be the friend of the widow. Dear Lord, I need You to be my friend."

So Anna entered into victory. She could have been bitter at the funeral. Instead she entered into the treasures of darkness. She decided she would make God's house her home.

The temple courts in Anna's day were both commodious and elaborate. The outer court, as rebuilt and extended by Herod, did not form a part of the sacred area. Gentiles were allowed to walk there so it was called the court of the Gentiles. The ruling religious authorities had concessions set up in this court. Their agents were always busy there changing money for buying and selling animals for sacrifices. Anna would make her way across this court until she came to some steps which led to a barrier.

This barrier was known as the middle wall of partition. On the wall notices in Greek and Latin were posted to warn Gentiles not to penetrate beyond that point. The penalty for not heeding this warning was death. Ritually unclean Jews were also forbidden to go beyond the wall. Nine massive gates led through this barrier. One of the gates, known as the beautiful gate, was sometimes called the Corinthian gate because it was overlaid with costly Corinthian bronze.

Anna would make her way through one of the gates and enter the court of the women. In this court the temple treasury was located. Jewish men could go farther—into the court of Israel. Descendants of Aaron could go farther still—into the court of the priests. Anna could go as far as the court of the women.

In this court she found a quiet corner that became her real

home. She "departed not from the temple," says the Holy Spirit (Luke 2:37). She made God her husband, she made His house her home, and she entered into the treasures of darkness. She said with Job, "Though he slay me, yet will I trust in him" (Job 13:15).

So instead of becoming bitter at the funeral, Anna dedicated her widowhood to God. She determined to be the happiest, holiest widow in Jerusalem.

B. Bitter over Her Family

Anna could have reacted against God even before she became a widow. She could have resented the fact that her parents made her go to the temple so often when she was a little girl. And then when tragedy struck she might have said, "If that's all the thanks I get for going to the temple all the time, that's it. I'll never darken the doors of the temple again." It is astonishing how many people offer excuses like that. Actually the most precious privilege ever granted to a human being is that of being born into a Christian home—a home where parents love the Lord, keep fellowship with God's people, require their children to go to Sunday school and church, and protect their children as far as possible from the ways of the world.

Think of it—one could have been born into a Hindu home. Until recently some little Hindu girls were subjected to the horrors of child marriage.[1] Others were destined to serve as temple prostitutes. Hindus have some 300 million gods, they worship idols, and they venerate rats and vermin. Some time ago *National Geographic* carried an illustrated article showing food actually being set out for the benefit of rats that are regarded as sacred—in a land that traditionally has had trouble feeding its millions of people.[2]

Or one could have been born into a Muslim home. Muslims are taught to worship Allah and to revere the teachings of a fierce and lustful prophet. Their creed revolves around the formula, "There is no god but Allah and Muhammad is his prophet."

Or one might have been born into a communist home. Communists indoctrinate their children in the lie that there is no God. Millions of communists die in their sins without God, without Christ, without hope—never having heard of John 3:16.

Those who are born into Christian homes are greatly privileged. Yet some resent their Christian upbringing and cannot wait to get away from it. Like the prodigal son they throw off the restraints and requirements of a godly home. They have been brought up surrounded by sublime truth. They have been taught that Jesus is the eternal uncreated Son of the living God, that He deliberately incarnated Himself in human form at Bethlehem, that He "went about doing good," that He lives in the power of an endless life, and that He is mighty to save. Yet they want to throw their heritage away.

When a person decides to turn his back on all that is Christian, God sometimes lets him. It will be more tolerable for some shivering naked cannibal standing at the great white throne on the day of judgment than for such a rebel.

Anna's father must have been a very godly man. His name was Phanuel, which means "the face of God." Anna grew up in a home where her father was a living image of God to her childish soul. She saw the face of God in the face of her father. She knew what God was like because she knew what her father was like.

My own father had his faults and failings like anyone else, but he showed me the face of God. I have never known another man who could pray like my father prayed. When my father stood up to lead God's people in prayer, he lifted them into the very throne room of the universe.

Why do so many Christian parents see their children go astray? Sometimes it is because the children look at their parents and do not see the face of God. Christian parents must do more than talk about what is right. Their supreme responsibility is to live Christ so that their children will think of the face of God whenever they think of their parents.

C. Bitter over Her Frailty

Even though Anna was not bitter over her family, she could have been bitter over her declining health. A person does not arrive at the age of approximately 110 without accumulating the inevitable physical consequences of old age. Perhaps she had arthritis or rheumatism. She might have had a weak heart or bad circulation. She could easily have pleaded her old age as an excuse for no longer going to the temple. But Anna's chief delight was to be where God's people came together.

Her friends might have said, "Granny, you'd better give it up. You could fall down and break your hip on those stairs." "Granny, you can't go to the house of God today. It's raining." "Granny, now that you're so old, why not ease up a little? Why not settle for the sabbath? Just go to the temple on the sabbath."

But Anna would have said, "I'm looking for the coming of the Lord, and when He comes I know where I want Him to find me. I can think of a thousand places where I don't want Him to find me. I know where I would like Him to find me; and I know where I'm most likely to find Him—in the temple. You'll never keep me away from God's house."

When Jesus was twelve years old and Mary and Joseph lost Him, they went back to Jerusalem and spent three days searching the city. Astonishingly, they never thought of looking in the temple. Yet Jesus had haunted that temple. Anna was like Jesus: she loved the place where God's people met. So did Peter and John. Acts 4:23 says that after they were threatened by the Sanhedrin, "being let go, [Peter and John] went to their own company." There is more truth than poetry in the old saying that birds of a feather flock together.

D. Bitter over Her Finances

Anna could have used her financial status as well as her frailty as an excuse for not going to the temple. There were vested interests in that temple. There were those who under the guise of religion fleeced the widows and the helpless. Jesus spoke of those charlatans who "devour widows' houses, and for a pretence make long prayers" (Mark 12:40).

Under Jewish law a widow could not dispose of her property except through the rabbis, some of whom were cheats. Quite possibly Anna herself had been cheated. But the fact that some people use religion as a cloak to cover up their wickedness made no difference to Anna. She was not going to let their hypocrisy rob her of her own joy in the Lord.

The Holy Spirit says of Anna that she "departed not from the temple" (Luke 2:37). The word *not* is strong, expressing full and direct negation: absolutely not. There were no ifs, ands, or buts: Anna lived solely for the place where God had put His name. Her whole life revolved around the temple.

A verse in Anna's Bible told her that the Lord would come suddenly into His temple (Malachi 3:1). She did not know where else He would come, but she knew He would come there. So the temple was where Anna wanted to be.

Anna triumphed over all the big and little excuses people make for staying away from the gathering place of the people of God. She was not infatuated by the temple itself, but she wanted to be where God Himself had promised to be. Her presence in the temple was evidence of her victory over bitterness.

II. HER VOCATION

Luke 2:37 tells us that this remarkable woman "served God with fastings and prayers night and day." The word translated "served" signifies "worshiped." Anna devoted her whole life to praying for the Lord's coming. She could see wrongs all about her, even in the temple, and she longed for the Lord to come and right those wrongs.

When we read of Anna's vocation we can picture an old woman, bent and feeble, *doing what the high priest should have been doing.* (The high priest, as everyone knew, was more interested in the politics of his office than anything else.) We can also picture an old woman *doing what the shining seraphim and cherubim are doing.* We see Anna, as the hymn says, "gazing on the Lord in glory." We see her day and night ceasing not to cry, "Holy, holy, holy, is the Lord. . . . Thou art worthy, O Lord, to receive glory and honour and power: for thou hast created all things, and for thy pleasure they are and were created" (Isaiah 6:3; Revelation 4:11).

Anna brought her body under control and she set her spirit free. Her life's work was to praise the Lord and to pray— for her family and friends, for the leaders of her nation, for the spiritual life of her people, for those who ruled the land, for God's kingdom to come, and for His will to be done on earth as it is in Heaven.

The name *Anna* (Hannah) means "God is gracious." People might have said to her, "God is gracious? He took away your husband in your youth when you had been married barely seven years. God is gracious?" But Anna would have said, "Oh yes! That was His gracious way of wedding me to Himself. Do you think I have been a widow these past eighty-four years? Oh no! I have been married to Another, even to Him who is to be raised from the dead."

Anna's vocation was to pray. God has few saints like her on earth. He has plenty of people who are willing to preach. He has only a few who are willing to pray, and even fewer who feel called to make prayer and fasting the great and controlling ministry of their lives.

III. HER VISION

One day Anna's prayers were answered!

The day began like any other day. Anna probably woke up that morning at the usual time. With her poor old bones and joints all stiff, she took a little while to get going. She dressed, went outside, picked up her pitcher, and hobbled down to the well. There she exchanged a few pleasantries with other women from the neighborhood. Then she went back home to make herself a little porridge for breakfast.

Taking her well-worn staff, off she went to the temple. She knew her way blindfolded; she knew every house and shop, every man and woman, every stick and stone.

She puffed and panted a little as she came to the temple mount. Rising from the deep valleys, the mount was like an island surrounded by a sea of walls, palaces, streets, and houses. Rising terrace after terrace, the mount was crowned by a mass of snowy marble and glittering gold. Anna paused to admire the splendor of the view. She had seen it thousands of times but it never failed to take her breath away. She had seen that gigantic sacred enclosure thronged with as many as two hundred thousand people on high days and holy days.

Once within the temple gates Anna saw colonnades and porches everywhere—the most famous was the ancient eastern colonnade known as Solomon's porch. She saw the pinnacle of the temple towering 450 feet above the Kidron valley.

Once past the colonnades she entered the court of the Gentiles. As she walked through she looked with disapproval at the way it had been turned into a market. Coming to the middle wall of partition she labored up the fourteen steps to enter, through one of the splendid gates, the court of the women. There Anna found her habitual corner and began her daily round of prayer.

But this day was different from any other day, for on this day Jesus came!

Anna noticed a man and a woman coming. They were obviously poor and had with them a baby wrapped in a blanket. Then Anna saw an old man approach them. She knew that old man. He was Simeon. She couldn't help overhearing what Simeon said as he intercepted the couple and took the baby in his arms: "Lord, now lettest thou thy servant depart in peace, according to thy word: For mine eyes have seen thy salvation" (Luke 2:29-30).

Anna's heart leaped. *It was the Lord! Hallelujah! He'd come! Of course! Of course! He was to come as a baby. A virgin was to conceive and bear a Son.* And Anna burst into thanksgiving and praise.

She now had a new vocation. She spoke of Him to all who looked for redemption in Jerusalem (Luke 2:38). She knew every believer in town. "He's here!" she would say to each and every one of them. "I've seen Him. His name is *Jesus.* Keep your eyes open. He'll be back in your lifetime. Be sure you are ready."

So instead of becoming bitter, Anna became a blessing. Anna's joy over the coming of Jesus is ample testimony to God's faithfulness in rewarding a life like hers.

---

1. What those horrors were has been amply documented in a harrowing book entitled *Mother India* by Katherine Mayo (New York: Harcourt, Brace, 1927).

2. *National Geographic,* July 1977, 71.

7
Ananias and Sapphira, the Biggest Liars

Acts 5:1-11

A *nanias* and *Sapphira*—the two names sound like music in our ears. The name *Ananias* means "Jehovah has graciously given." It reminds us of words from an old hymn:

> Savior, Thy dying love
> Thou gavest me,
> Nor should I aught withhold,
> Dear Lord, from Thee.
>
> . . . .

All that I am and have,
Thy gifts so free,
In joy, in grief, thro' life,
Dear Lord, for Thee!
(Sylvanus D. Phelps)

Sapphira, an Aramaic word, simply means "beautiful." One name captures the thought of *bounty;* the other captures the thought of *beauty.* If the pair had lived up to their names, they would have been permanent ornaments of the church— enduring examples of the bounty and beauty of the Lord Jesus. Instead they were a pair of Achans in the camp (Joshua 7). Like their Old Testament counterpart, they perished under the judgment hand of God.

The Holy Spirit associates the story of Ananias and Sapphira with three expressions: "great power," "great grace," and "great fear." In other words, this story provides lessons in discipleship, fellowship, and membership.

I. A LESSON IN DISCIPLESHIP: Great Power

The story of Ananias and Sapphira was told in the context of a description of the early church. Let us consider the men who established the church and the power of their message.

A. The Men

"With great power gave the apostles witness" (Acts 4:33). The apostles themselves were ordinary men. In fact the Sanhedrin contemptuously called them "unlearned and ignorant" (4:13). *What under the sun,* thought the Jewish religious leaders, *is there to fear from a dozen fishermen, tax collectors, and peasants? Why, there isn't a single educated man among them. They are not rich. They are not sophisticated. They are not from the upper crust of society. They are common Galileans.* But the apostles had been with Jesus! That was the secret of their power. What distinguished the apostles from other men was the amount of time they had spent in the personal company of the Lord Jesus.

It is almost redundant to say that we do not have apostles in the church today. The gift of the apostle was special and specialized. The nursery no longer exists where apostles can be born and raised. John lived longer than any of the other apostles and when he died, the office of the apostle died.

The word *apostle,* however, simply means "sent one." There are many "sent ones" today. Indeed, all Christians are "sent ones." The *work* of the apostle remains though the *gift* of the apostle has ceased.

The early apostles had spent time with the Son of God and had been baptized, indwelt, sealed, filled, and anointed by the Spirit of God. In the sense that anyone can become acquainted with the Son of God and make himself available to the Spirit of God, anyone can be an apostle. That is the kind of man God uses to build His church. In the early days the Jerusalem church was uniquely blessed in that it had about a dozen such men in its ranks.

B. The Message

The early church had only one message: Christ—alive from the dead, ascended on high, seated at God's right hand, and coming again. "With great power gave the apostles witness of the resurrection of the Lord Jesus" (Acts 4:33).

The resurrection of Christ is the one great irrefutable argument for Christianity. During the French revolution a Frenchman named Lepeaux was disappointed in the poor success he was having in launching a new religion, which to his mind was far superior to Christianity. He appealed to Charles Maurice de Tallyrand, a statesman-bishop who became a leader of the godless French revolution. Lepeaux asked Tallyrand, "What should I do to get my plans off the ground?" "My dear M. Lepeaux," the statesman said, "it is a very difficult thing to start a new religion. But there is one thing you might at least try. I suggest you get yourself crucified and then rise again on the third day."

The resurrection was the dynamic of the apostles' message, and of course it is gloriously true. "God hath raised him from the dead," wrote Paul to the Romans (Romans 10:9).

Eusebius, an early church father and historian, told us that when the news began to circulate in Jerusalem that Jesus Christ was alive from the dead, Pontius Pilate, the Roman governor, considered the story to be of sufficient importance that he officially referred the matter to Tiberius. Under Roman law the Roman senate had the authority to rule on all claims to deity. Eusebius wrote: "An ancient law prevailed that no one should be made a God by the Romans except by a vote and decree of the Senate. The Senate rejected the Nazarene's claim to deity" (*Ecclesiastical History,* Book 2, chapter 2). Apparently the Lord Jesus did not think it worthwhile to get the Romans' approval before claiming to be God and proving it by rising from the dead!

The well-publicized case of Lord Lyttleton and Gilbert West illustrates the power of the apostles' message. These two men, unbelieving and skeptical, decided that the best way to overthrow Christianity was to undermine belief in its two cardinal historical facts: the resurrection of Christ and the conversion of the apostle Paul. Lyttleton undertook to discredit the account of the conversion of Paul and West undertook to disprove the resurrection of Christ. When meeting to discuss their progress, they made a great discovery: they had both been so convinced by the evidence that they had written their books to prove the opposite of what they had set out to prove. Some years ago I checked West's book out of the Moody Bible Institute library and read its clear message of a Christ who died, was buried, and rose again.

For a number of years Allan Redpath was the pastor of Moody Memorial Church in Chicago. At one Moody Bible Institute Founders Week Conference I heard him use the following illustration in a sermon.

It seems that Redpath was an Englishman and though he had lived in the United States for a long time, he retained his love for English sports. He was especially interested in the annual cricket test match (the highest level of competition) between England and Australia. But he could find few people in the United States who even knew what cricket was and still fewer who cared anything about the test match.

The match began each day at 11:00 a.m., stopped at 1:00 p.m. for lunch, resumed at 1:45 p.m., stopped at 3:30 p.m. for tea (cricket is a gentlemanly sport), resumed at 4:00 p.m., and stopped at 6:30 p.m. Each year the match went on like that for five days.

One year when Redpath was living in Chicago, he wanted to know how the annual match was going. He bought every Chicago newspaper he could lay his hands on but he couldn't find a word about the match. The American journalists were only interested in the Cubs and the Sox. So a friend from England kindly airmailed him a copy of a London paper. The headline on the front page was "England Facing Defeat." This news was more depressing than no news at all. Worse still, nobody seemed to care. But two days later Redpath received another British newspaper. This time the headline read, "England In Sight Of Victory." In two days the whole situation had changed.

Likewise it was a sad day at Calvary when Joseph took Jesus down from the cross, wrapped His body in graveclothes, and put Him in a tomb. The world went on its way. Few people cared. But the disciples were utterly demoralized and defeated. Thomas became an avowed skeptic, Peter ate his heart out with remorse, and John did his best to comfort the Lord's mother Mary. Then came the resurrection morning! In three days the whole situation had changed.

That was the point of Redpath's illustration and that was the message of the early church: the whole situation had changed. And the news spread. As Paul said to King Agrippa, "This thing was not done in a corner" (Acts 26:26). Peter, James,

John, Matthew, Thomas, and all the rest of the disciples were eyewitnesses of the risen Christ. Their powerful message would turn the world upside down.

II. A LESSON IN FELLOWSHIP: Great Grace

Adding to his description of the early church, Luke said, "Great grace was upon them all" (Acts 4:33). That outstanding characteristic and quality of life which marked the Christ now marked the Christians. The overflow of love among Christians was such that a brother who had money in the bank would share his money with a brother in great need. Before long the prevailing custom was share and share alike. This generous lifestyle was an experiment in pure socialism—that is, socialism based on the utmost ideal and motivated by what the Holy Spirit calls "great grace." The experiment did not last and it did not work, but it was an interesting attempt to have all things in common.

Acts 4:36-37 gives us the example of Barnabas. He was a Levite who owned property on the island of Cyprus. Carried away with the spirit of the early church, this "son of consolation" sold his property and put the proceeds at the apostles' feet. The Holy Spirit neither approves nor disapproves the deed. He simply cites it as an example of the overflowing love and fellowship of the early church.

This kind of socialism is neither commanded nor commended in the Epistles. The noble experiment was simply recorded as a phase through which the early church passed. Before long, abuses arose and Jerusalem was known far and wide for its poor saints. There was never enough to go around.

Brief though it was, the early experiment in sharing is a lesson in fellowship. Although the Holy Spirit does not require a Christian with means to beggar himself in order to help the poor, He certainly does expect the Christian to be concerned about the physical and material needs of the less fortunate.

"The poor always ye have with you," Jesus said (John 12:8). We can find plenty of outlets for our generosity if we have the compassion of Christ in our hearts.

Caring for the sick, the poor, the orphaned, the aged, and the illiterate has always been and still is one of the great concerns of the church. The early church was very much alive to the needs of the unfortunate and the poor. Always a leader in social reform, the church built the first hospitals, asylums, orphan homes, and rescue missions. But the modern church has surrendered half its mission to the government. Such surrender leads to socialism without a soul and a welfare state without a conscience.

The gospel of Christ always quickens the conscience of the individual so that he becomes aware of the social ills of mankind. For example, Lord Shaftesbury, a Christian, became aware of the plight of little children working like slaves to feed the jaw of the "Moloch" of Britain's industrial machine and started a campaign against this injustice. William Wilberforce, a Christian, aroused a lethargic British parliament to abolish slavery throughout the empire. George Muller, a Christian, reached out to the destitute orphans in England's streets. Amy Wilson Carmichael, a missionary to India, gave impetus to helping wretched widows and rescuing little children destined for prostitution in Hindu temples. And the early Christians were aware of each other's needs and "distribution was made unto every man according as he had need" (Acts 4:35).

After describing the generosity that characterized the early church, Luke told the story of Ananias and Sapphira.

III. A LESSON IN MEMBERSHIP: Great Fear

The facts behind the story are that two great protagonists came to the floor of the church. Satan came to battle the Spirit of God. God demonstrated His power and great fear came upon the church.

What Ananias and Sapphira did is linked by a conjunction

to what Barnabas had done. They had been impressed by his gift. They had particularly liked the applause that, all unsought and unwanted, he had received. His gift seems to have been exceptionally generous since the Holy Spirit draws such special attention to it. Anyway, Ananias and Sapphira had a family conference and decided to emulate the generosity of Barnabas. Acts 5:1 says they "sold a possession."

But Acts 5:2 says they "kept back part of the price." Within a stone's throw of Pentecost Ananias and Sapphira entered into an agreement to deceive. (Deception is Satan's favorite device.) Their fall into sin was not sudden. Ananias and Sapphira were not overwhelmed by temptation. Their deception was planned and deliberate.

When Ananias and Sapphira sold the property, the proceeds were more than they expected. "We don't have to give it all," they agreed. Later when Peter demanded an explanation from Sapphira he said, "How is it that ye have agreed together to tempt the Spirit of the Lord?" (Acts 5:9) Peter used the word *sumphoneo* from which our word "symphony" is derived. Evidently Ananias and Sapphira shared a harmony of purpose. (The word *sumphoneo* is used in Acts 15:15 to describe the harmony of the Old and New Testament Scriptures: "To this agree the words of the prophets.")

Little did Ananias and Sapphira realize that there was an unseen listener to their whispered pact.

"How much did you get, Ananias?" we can hear Sapphira say.

"Twice what I asked for," we can hear Ananias reply. "The man wanted the land badly. He wants to build a bank on the corner. It's right near the temple."

"Do you think we have to give it all?"

"How about if we give all we originally intended and keep back the extra?"

"That's a good idea, Ananias. Do we need to tell anybody what the real market price was? It was a cash deal, wasn't it?"

"Yes, my friend wanted to deal in cash."

"Well, that's all right then. We'll tell everyone that we got such-and-such a price."

The unseen listener knew the market price. The Holy Spirit was there when the deal was struck. He knew to whom the property was sold and for how much. And He did not keep the information to Himself. He went and told Peter.

If the Savior detested one sin more than any other when He trod these scenes of time, that sin was hypocrisy. Honest doubts never angered Him, but He scathingly denounced hypocrisy. He who was and is the truth never made peace with a lie. Nor has His Holy Spirit.

Pretending to a holiness and a generosity they lacked, Ananias and Sapphira lied to the Holy Ghost and "kept back" *(nosphizomai)* part of the price (Acts 5:2-3). Note that Greek expression. When the translators of the Septuagint came to the story of Achan they used an almost identical word. They recorded that "the children of Israel committed a trespass in the accursed thing: for Achan . . . took *[enosphisanto]* of the accursed thing" (Joshua 7:1). This Greek expression means "took for himself." Achan hindered the blessing of God and so did Ananias and Sapphira. Their sin was covetousness, the love of money. They held on to what had been promised to God.

The Spirit of God acted at once. He did something Jesus never did—He smote. Once, twice, and two of God's people lay dead on the floor. That morning they had been wrapped in smug complacency. Before the day was done they were lying in their coffins.

How swiftly and terribly Ananias and Sapphira were exposed. Their story is a preview of the judgment seat of Christ. Never once did Peter question their salvation. The church has no business judging people who are "without"—only those who are "within" (1 Corinthians 5:12).

Now let's backtrack to an earlier point in the story. Ananias laid his offering at the apostles' feet just as Barnabas had done. "Well bless you, my brother," we can hear Peter say. "This is a generous sum. I take it this is the full price you received for the property?" Ananias could have told the truth. He could have said, "No, as a matter of fact I did get more for the land but I decided to keep some of the proceeds for our own needs." That would have been perfectly acceptable (Acts 5:4). The Lord is not against private ownership of property.

The Lord said, "Sell all that thou hast, and distribute unto the poor" (Luke 18:22), but this is the counsel of perfection. It is not an obligation. It is not a necessary part of being a believer. It is not an evidence of grace. The idea of "lordship salvation" is not found in the New Testament. We must not confuse conversion with consecration. Selling all that we have and giving it to the poor is an evidence of growth, not grace. In the case of the rich young ruler, the Lord saw that his love of money was a stumbling block to his salvation.

Ananias was a free agent as far as his property was concerned. He could keep it, sell it, give all of it away, or give part of it away. There was no physical necessity, church necessity, or spiritual necessity for him to sell the property and give any of the proceeds away. The only compulsion was love—the compulsion to be like Jesus, to express the compassion of Christ for the poor, to lay up treasure in Heaven.

Ananias could have told the truth, but he told his lie and judgment fell. "Thou hast not lied unto men," Peter said, "but unto God" (Acts 5:4). The man dropped dead on the spot and within an hour he was in his tomb.

Three hours later his wife came in. Where had she been the past three hours? Maybe she'd gone to the bank to deposit the nice little nest egg they had left over. Perhaps she had been in the market deciding how to spend the extra money. Possibly she had been at home waiting for Ananias to return and had decided to go to the church to see if he were there.

Anyway, Sapphira came in all smiles. By now their generous gift would be the talk of the church. She nodded to this one and that one. Too eager to receive the praise of men, she did not notice the strained silence. Casually Peter asked her the fateful question. The interrogation probably went like this:

"By the way, Sapphira, how much did you get for that piece of property? Ananias was here a little while ago. He did mention a price. Do I have the figure right? Was it such and such?"

Apparently Sapphira took no alarm at Peter's question. She was so preoccupied with material things that she failed to detect the tenseness of the atmosphere and the pointedness of the question. Or did she suspect something at the last moment, but tried to protect her husband?

Alarmed or not, Sapphira answered Peter's question with a barefaced lie and her doom was swift. Peter's terrible words fell on her ears: "How is it that ye have agreed together to tempt the Spirit of the Lord? behold, the feet of them which have buried thy husband are at the door, and shall carry thee out" (Acts 5:9). She had no time for reflection, no time for repentance. Caught red-handed lying to the Spirit of God, she dropped dead at Peter's feet.

"Great fear came upon all the church" (Acts 5:11). Suddenly people woke up to the fact that the church was a place of terrifying holiness. Fear fell on the unsaved and on those who came to church for the loaves and fishes (the fringe benefits of Christianity). Nobody dared join the church (5:13).

Nowadays almost anyone can join most churches—the only requirement for membership is a letter of transfer, a glib profession of faith, or an agreement to get baptized. Why does not God's judgment fall today? People get away with lying to the Holy Spirit. They promise to tithe, teach a Sunday school class, study their Bibles, go to the mission field, or visit the sick. Then they break their promises and nothing happens.

In contrast to many churches today, the early church was energized by great power, great grace, and great fear. If the church of today had the *dynamic* of the church of that day, it would have the *discipline* of that day. And if the church of today had the *discipline* of that day, it would have the *dynamic* of that day.

8
Herod Agrippa I, the Meanest Murderer

Acts 12:1-25

> ## I. THE HOLLOW CROWN
> ## II. THE HIDEOUS CRIME
> ### A. The Death of James
> ### B. The Detention of Peter
> ## III. THE HAUGHTY CLAIM

H erod Agrippa I wielded a murderous hand at the helm. He was a scheming, grasping, treacherous individual. The Herods were a bad lot. They were true children of Esau, Edomites with hands dyed red with the blood of innocent men, women, boys, and girls. Disregarding the laws of God or man, the Herods were a law unto themselves. A man would be better off trusting a rattlesnake than trusting a Herod. The family was not without wit, charm, and genius. Herod the so-called Great was a magnificent builder, bold ruler, and crafty negotiator. But woe would betide the man who crossed a

Herod, or who had something a Herod wanted, or who stood in a Herod's way.

Herod Agrippa I, whom we meet in the early chapters of Acts, is not the Herod we meet in the Gospels. The man who murdered John and mocked at Jesus was Herod Antipas, an uncle of Herod Agrippa I.

I. THE HOLLOW CROWN

The Herods thought they were big men, but they were only as big as God in Heaven and caesar on earth allowed them to be. Nevertheless they made plenty of noise and threw their weight around in their own small puddles. If you'd heard them talk and seen them strut, you'd have thought they ruled the world, not just bits and pieces of a little land held in Rome's iron hand. A Herod's crown was hollow.

The grandfather of Herod Agrippa I was Herod the Great, the big-time builder. One of his projects was the temple in Jerusalem. It took about eighty-four years to build the temple, and about six years after it was completed it was destroyed by the Romans in accordance with the words of Christ. The Roman general Titus had ordered it to be preserved. Jesus had declared it would be razed. Jesus proved to be right.

Another landmark of Herod the Great's building genius was the Roman city of Caesarea on the coastline of his realm. Caesarea was an architectural marvel because its builders had to overcome enormous obstacles when constructing the harbor.

Herod the Great, however, is best known to us as the one who murdered the babes of Bethlehem in an effort to destroy the newborn Christ of God.

The grandmother of Herod Agrippa I was the beautiful Mariamne. Herod the Great was madly in love with this princess, yet that did not stop him from murdering her and her two brothers. After that he became insane. His nights were haunted by the beautiful woman he had married and murdered and his days were spent trying to find another woman like her.

On one occasion he saw a woman of the streets who reminded him of his dead princess. Despite all warnings, he wanted her. He got what he wanted and contracted a foul disease that rotted his body through and through.

The father of Herod Agrippa I was Aristobulus, who was also murdered by his father Herod the Great. Agrippa's parents were first cousins. Agrippa himself was married to his first cousin, the daughter of an aunt who was married to an uncle. No wonder there was a trace of madness in the Herods.

When Herod the Great murdered Aristobulus in a fit of jealous rage, Agrippa was sent off to Rome by his mother so that he would be out of the reach of his evil grandfather. No wonder Caesar Augustus said it was better to be Herod the Great's hog than his son.

Agrippa's uncle Philip married the bloodthirsty Herodias. Then Agrippa's uncle Antipas ran away with Herodias. Agrippa's cousin Salome (daughter of Herodias) performed a provocative dance before her stepfather Antipas and so inflamed the lustful king that he promised her half his kingdom. She settled instead, under the urging of her she-wolf mother, to demand the head of John the Baptist on a platter.

Agrippa's brother Herod of Chalcis married his niece Berenice. Later on Berenice showed up as the consort of her brother Agrippa II under circumstances that caused the tongues of the scandalmongers to wag.

Such was the Herod family. They had little or no moral scruples. The only law they consulted was the law of their own lustful desires.

While the young Herod Agrippa I was in Rome he made an important friend. That friend was Gaius, the grandnephew of Tiberius Caesar. Gaius is better known today as Caligula. When Tiberius died, Caligula became the emperor. Caligula remembered his friend Agrippa and sent him back to Palestine as king. Later on the emperor Claudius enlarged the domains of Herod Agrippa I so that he actually ruled a kingdom almost as large as that of his grandfather Herod the Great.

However, the crown was hollow. The king who wore it could never forget that he was, after all, a puppet of the caesar. When Agrippa was on his way back to Palestine, he stopped in Alexandria, Egypt. There the Greeks openly mocked and derided him. Nor was he greatly liked by his subjects. He was too much the child of Roman vice, too much given to Greek frivolity, too glib with his lip service to Judaism, too much a savage Herod, and too much an Idumean.

So Herod Agrippa I wore a crown, but it commanded little or no respect from the Jews. True, he could claim descent from Mariamne, daughter of an ancient line of Jewish priest-kings. But the wild blood of Esau ran too strongly in the veins of the Herods for any of them to be able to command much respect in the Jewish promised land. Agrippa, however, sought to make friends among the Jews when he could. He was an old hand at buttering the toast of those who wielded real power. He played up to Caiaphas, Annas, and the college of Jewish cardinals who sat in the Sanhedrin and pulled important strings.

II. THE HIDEOUS CRIME

Agrippa was politician enough to know that if he wanted to gain favor with Caiaphas and his crowd, he must side with them against the church. Most of the Sanhedrin viewed the church with hatred. They hated Christ. They hated the ignorant and unlearned men who were fast rendering Judaism obsolete. Caiaphas and his friends resented the success of the handful of Galilean fishermen who were winning thousands of converts to Christ. The Jewish leaders resented the boldness of the Christians and their complete indifference to the commands and threats issued by the Sanhedrin.

It did not take Agrippa long to put two and two together. A good way to ingratiate himself with the Jewish authorities would be to do their dirty work for them. Having no scruples, he acted to please the Sanhedrin.

A. The Death of James

"Now about that time [about the time that Paul and Barnabas showed up with a substantial cash donation from the dynamic Gentile church in Antioch for the support of poor Christians in Jerusalem] Herod the king stretched forth his hands to vex certain of the church. And he killed James the brother of John with the sword" (Acts 12:1-2). The Greek word translated "vex," *kakoō,* means "to do evil to someone, especially to harm physically or maltreat someone." In the case of James the maltreatment took the form of coldblooded murder—premeditated and malicious. Herod acted without any cause or provocation, but he thought he could get away with the crime because he sat in a seat of dictatorial power.

James had been a Galilean fisherman. He and his brother John were first cousins of Jesus. James' mother was one of the Lord's most devoted followers and accompanied Him even to the cross. At the call of Jesus, James and John left their fishing business and became the Lord's most intimate disciples. James was one of the three disciples chosen by Jesus to witness the raising of Jairus's daughter, to be present on the mount of transfiguration, and to watch and pray with Him in the garden of Gethsemane.

We can well imagine that in the infant church James was much in demand as a speaker. New converts would be eager to hear him tell over and over again of the many marvelous and mighty works of Jesus. He would recount for them firsthand the sermon on the mount, the Olivet discourse, and the many parables. He would tell how Jesus cleansed lepers, gave sight to the blind, fed multitudes, and raised the dead.

James would tell them with an embarrassed laugh how he and John had persuaded their mother to ask Jesus to give them high posts of honor in His kingdom (Matthew 20:21-28). "How little we understood about the kingdom in those days," he would say. He would look around the group and add: "Jesus answered, 'Ye know not what ye ask. Are ye able to drink of the cup that I shall drink of, and to be baptized with the baptism that I am baptized with?' We boasted that we could. Well, He gave us a chance to taste of that cup when He took us to Gethsemane, and we fell asleep. We had the chance to follow Him to Golgotha, and we ran away."

So James went quietly about his business, telling the story of Jesus to this person and that group until he filled Jerusalem with the knowledge of Christ. James' testimony was so effective that when Herod decided to vex the church, he thought it would be a good idea to get rid of James first. Thus James became the first martyr among the apostles. Herod simply ordered his henchmen to execute James and then the king sat back to reap the approval and applause of the Jewish religious elite.

B. The Detention of Peter

"Because he saw it [James' death] pleased the Jews, he proceeded further to take Peter also" (Acts 12:3). Peter was taken on the anniversary of Christ's murder. It was the feast of unleavened bread, which is closely associated with Passover. Herod was delighted with the new friendliness of the Jewish high priest and his toadies. Arresting Peter was a cheap and easy way to keep the troublesome Sanhedrin happy and content.

Herod doubtless imprisoned Peter in the strongly garrisoned fortress of Antonia, which frowned down on the temple court. Peter was locked up as tightly as any prisoner today on death row. Between him and freedom stood two iron chains, sixteen soldiers, various keepers, and an iron gate. Four relays of soldiers guarded him around the clock. There were four guards in each relay. Two of the guards stood at the door. The other two guards stood one on either side of him; doubtless, in keeping with Roman custom, Peter was actually chained to these two. Moreover, the death sentence had been signed and would be carried out the next day.

So what did Peter do? Did he pray, pleading with God to

set him free? (God had given him the keys of the kingdom, but a lot of good they were doing him now.) Did he pace the floor of his cell, grit his teeth, and bravely resolve to die like a man? Did he ask God to give him dying grace? No. He simply committed his soul to God, said goodnight to his jailers, and went to sleep! He was not just a conqueror; he was more than a conqueror.

Peter had already learned how to be crucified with Christ. The life that he now lived he lived by the faith of the Son of God (Galatians 2:20). To Peter death was simply a matter of being absent from the body and present with the Lord (2 Corinthians 5:8).

We can imagine what the angel who visited Peter in his cell said when he reported back to the courts of bliss. "What was Peter doing when I arrived? Bless you, he was sound asleep! I had to give him quite a blow to wake him up. You'd have thought he was safe and sound in his own bed."

Meanwhile the church was praying. The church knew how to pray in those days. Luke wrote, "But prayer was made without ceasing of the church unto God for him" (Acts 12:5). Peter was asleep but his brothers in Christ were wide awake. Across Jerusalem and up and down Judea all-night prayer meetings were in progress. The court of Heaven was being bombarded and blitzed by an enormous barrage of intercessory prayer.

The church could not imagine itself without big, blustering, bossy, beloved Peter. He had such a happy knack of putting his foot in his mouth and making people love him for it. God had used Peter to perform miracles. Peter was the one who preached on the day of Pentecost, the birthday of the church. Peter was the one who was speaking when the Holy Ghost was given to the Samaritans. Peter had flung wide the door of the church to the Gentiles. Peter was always way out in front of everyone else or lagging his feet far behind. Peter could tell inimitable stories about Jesus. Peter was famous for his bluff honesty; he would shout a person down one moment and weep with sorrow and regret the next. Peter had bravely faced the Sanhedrin. Peter was one of the chosen three, along with James and John, who knew Jesus best. The church could not imagine itself without Peter, so the church prayed.

On the surface it seemed as if all the odds were with Herod Agrippa I. He had the fortress and the soldiers, the power and the authority. He had the confidence of the caesar and the great seal to legitimize his actions. Behind Herod stood imperial Rome and its armies of iron. Alongside Herod stood the powerful Sanhedrin, which spoke for hundreds of thousands of Jews at home and abroad.

On the other hand there was a praying church—ordinary men, women, boys, and girls who loved Jesus. An unsaved betting man would have put his money on Herod, especially after the martyrdom of James. The God of the Christians had not lifted a finger to help him.

Then the miracle happened. Down from the heights of Heaven came Peter's angel. How we would like to know more about these angels! We each have one. Peter and Paul saw theirs. Little children have angels. Individual churches have angels.

Jacob's ladder swarms with angels. In Genesis 28 we see them ascending and descending that shining stairway. They trudge upwards weighed down with the sad stories of man's injustices, atrocities, and downright wickedness. They come back down refreshed and revived, their eyes alight with new resolve; they are returning to earth with new orders from the throne of God.

Peter's angel came to the jail. What cared the angel for iron gates and iron men? A snap of his fingers and all the guards were sound asleep. An imperious beckoning of his hand and Peter followed. (Peter, dazed and still half asleep, thought he was having a particularly interesting and vivid dream.) The door swung open of its own accord. The iron gate felt a sudden impulse to fling itself open. The gate let the great apostle of the Lamb pass and then shut itself again with a triumphant clang.

The night air smelled sweet and fresh after the fetid atmosphere of the prison. Peter turned around to thank his benefactor but he was gone! Peter was free—but by no means safe. God never does for us what we can do for ourselves, so Peter set off for the house of Mary, the mother of John Mark. Mary's house was one of the primary meeting places of the Jerusalem church.

We have all chuckled over what happened next. Rhoda, who couldn't believe that Peter was really at the door, left him standing there while she ran in to tell the news to the people who had gathered to pray. It was incredible. God had answered prayer! "It's his angel!" said the people (Acts 12:15). But Peter's persistent banging on the door at last produced the desired result. We can imagine the hubbub in that house.

Peter prudently decided to go into hiding before the morning came and off he went into the night. As for Herod, he simply added to his other crimes by ordering the execution of Peter's unoffending guards.

III. THE HAUGHTY CLAIM

Herod went back to Caesarea after all this "and there abode," the Holy Spirit says (Acts 12:19). The Greek word translated "abode," *diatribō*, literally means "to rub away, to spend time." Herod went on rubbing away the little bit of time he had left.

Then a crisis arose in the coastal cities of Tyre and Sidon, old Phoenician trading centers. Herod exerted pressure, things came to a head, and the cities gave in. When the cities sent a delegation to Caesarea to make their peace with the royal tyrant, Herod decided to make an occasion out of it. He would accept the surrender with suitable festivities and all due pomp and circumstance.

On the second day of the festivities Herod decided to make an especially grand entrance. He put on a gorgeous robe woven throughout with strands of silver. He entered the theater where everyone was assembled at the break of day so that the first rays of the rising sun would shine on him. His robe blazed and flashed as though with fire and the people cried out, "This is a god!"

Then the watching angel smote him. As Herod drank in the adulation of his subjects, God summoned worms to gnaw at his intestines. Five days later he died in agony. The invisible watcher made his report; the invisible worm did his work. Herod was only fifty-four. He had been king for less than seven years.

The judgment of God is not always that obvious but it is always certain. We may not see the immediate sequence of cause and effect, but we can be sure that it is there.

Herod Agrippa I was dead and damned "but the word of God grew and multiplied" (Acts 12:24). The Word of God lived on. It lives on still, and will live on and on even when time will be no more. God buries the opposition, and His work and His Word go on.

9
Philip, the Busiest Deacon

Acts 6:2-5; 8:5-40

```
I. THE CLAN
II. THE MAN
III. THE PLAN
```

Theree was a problem in the Jerusalem church—too many apostles in too small a space. They were all there. Their horizons began and ended in Jerusalem, their native Galilee, and surrounding Judea. The Lord's last words had been plain enough: "Ye shall be witnesses unto me both in Jerusalem, and in all Judaea, and in Samaria, and unto the uttermost part of the earth" (Acts 1:8). But no one took these words seriously, except Philip—and he wasn't even an apostle.

I. THE CLAN

In those days Christianity was clannish. One had to be a Jew to get into the church. One had to subscribe to a temple-oriented, ritual-related, legalistically-leavened form of Christianity. Peter endorsed that idea, as did James. Even though James was a latecomer, the fact that he had been the Lord's brother gave him special leverage within the Jerusalem church. James was a born legalist, a dedicated ascetic, and a convinced *Jewish* Christian. The other Christians were all intimidated by James.

The church was a Jewish church. The central and pivotal point of gathering was the temple. Christians tried to keep the peace with the Sanhedrin, the synagogue, and the sanctuary. The martyrdom of Stephen had rocked the boat; Christians had to be careful. They tried not to do anything that would cause offense.

The church, let it be said, was a big clan because a great many Jews had become Christians. That is, they had become Jewish Christians—law-keeping, circumcision-advocating, Sabbath-observing Christians. In their minds Christianity was just another form of Judaism, albeit an elevated and enlightened form. A great many priests had become Christians and the Pharisees were inclined to lean toward a Christianity that upheld the Mosaic law.

Peter, James, John, Thomas, Matthew, Philip, Nathanael, and the rest of the apostles were at the heart of the clan. We can be sure they were all very busy because there were thousands of people in the Jerusalem church alone.

Doubtless the apostles were popular speakers. They would be in demand for all kinds of meetings: gatherings in the temple courts, meetings for teaching doctrine, meetings for fellowship, meetings for breaking of bread, prayer meetings, home meetings, and baptisms. Many people would want to hear the authentic story of Jesus firsthand from those who had spent three and one-half years in His company.

The apostles were the proper custodians of the gospel. They could describe the Lord's many miracles and recount His wonderful teachings word for word. They knew His parables, His famous sermon on the mount, His Olivet discourse, and His teaching in the upper room by heart. None of Christ's words had as yet been written down, so the memories of the apostles were vital.

So the apostles were kept busy enough speaking. And it was still the age of miracles. Was anyone sick? Let him call for an apostle. Gifts of healing were still part of the accrediting phenomena of an apostle. Peter had even raised the dead.

The apostles would receive messages from all over the country. "Can Peter come to Capernaum and preach in the synagogue for the next three sabbaths?" "Can John come to Joppa? A brother here is desperately ill." "Can Thomas come to Tiberius and tell how the Lord convinced him that the resurrection was real?" Invitations kept pouring in. How could the apostles respond to these calls when they could hardly keep up with the work in Jerusalem?

The social side of the gospel continued to be somewhat of a headache also. The poor seemed to be getting poorer. There was no longer any question of unfairness in the distribution of funds, but there never seemed to be enough money to go around.

The church was all very correct, very conservative, very clannish, very careful, and reasonably comfortable. But God never intended for the apostles to be comfortable. He intended for them to get going to the ends of the earth. A ship tied up in harbor is usually very safe. But ships are built for the high seas—for breasting angry waves and defying storms.

The clan had comfortably forgotten the words of the Master (Acts 1:8). The apostles had evangelized Jerusalem and Judea and were content. Actually Jerusalem and Judea had more or less evangelized themselves. With the tremendous impetus of Pentecost the gospel had quickly spread over the homeland. But what about Samaria?

We can imagine the apostles themselves discussing that question. Jude the obscure might have said, "What about Samaria? Aren't we supposed to evangelize Samaria? That would be a good job for you, Peter. You always seem to like the lead and the limelight. Why don't you take the lead and go to Samaria?"

Peter would say, "Well I like that! Don't you people forget

that I'm the apostle to the circumcision. John, you wanted to call down fire on Samaria some years ago. Now's your chance. Go and call down some Pentecostal fire on Samaria. You're just the man for the job."

John would reply, "I don't feel any leading in that direction at all. Thomas, you're a converted skeptic. That would be a good place for you to go. We all know how skeptical the Samaritans would be if one of us Jews showed up and offered to be friendly. As a cured skeptic you'd be just the man to break down their barriers."

Thomas would say, "Thanks for nothing. Matthew's the man for that job, it seems to me. After all he was a tax collector at one time. He had no scruples in those days, so scruples shouldn't bother him now. We Jews have scruples about the Samaritans. Evangelizing *them* would be a good job for Matthew."

We can hear Matthew reply, "Let's put our hands on Simon the Zealot. What a marvelous job for him!"

Finally the Holy Spirit left them to their complacent inaction and turned to one of the new deacons instead. He said in effect, "Come on, Philip. You come with me. You and I will go on down to Samaria. We'll show them how it's done."

So Philip went to Samaria and revival broke out. Lives were transformed. Miracles happened. People were saved. The whole place turned upside down. "And the people *with one accord,*" Luke said, "gave heed" (Acts 8:6, italics added). Luke said the same thing of the disciples when just before Pentecost they were in the upper room eagerly awaiting the coming of the Holy Spirit: "They were all with one accord" (Acts 2:1).

There was great joy in Samaria (Acts 8:8) and there was great joy when the Welsh revival broke out. G. Campbell Morgan recorded his impression of the Welsh revival: "No song books, but ah, me! I nearly wept tonight over the singing of our last hymn. No choir did I say? It was all choir. And hymns! I stood and listened with wonder and amazement as the congregation sang hymn after hymn without hymn books. No advertising. The thing advertises itself. All over the country people were converted just by reading the newspaper accounts."

Revival came to Samaria and sure enough the devil had his counterfeit all ready and waiting, a scoundrel by the name of Simon Magus. All sorts of extraordinary and extrabiblical stories are told about Simon Magus.[1] It was said that he could make statues walk. He could roll himself in fire without being burned. He could turn stones into loaves, open bolted doors, melt iron, and produce phantoms at banquets. He could cause vessels in his house to move about and wait on him at the dinner table. Probably mesmerism was involved. Still, the stories circulated and continued after his apostasy.

Simon Magus was fascinated by the power of the Holy Ghost displayed by Philip. In fact Simon made a profession of faith in Christ and was baptized. It must have been the talk of the town. "Have you heard about Simon the sorcerer?"

"No, what has he done now?"

"He has become a Christian. He has been baptized. Can you believe it? They say he sits right up front at all the preacher's meetings."

Meanwhile the news of the revival in Samaria filtered back to Jerusalem and made its belated impact on the clan. The apostles decided they must get involved and sent both Peter and John.

Inevitably Simon met Simon. Simon Magus watched with astonishment as the Samaritan believers received the Holy Ghost when Simon Peter laid his hands on them. The laying on of hands was a method that was essential in the case of the Samaritans. The centuries-long animosity between the Jews and Samaritans made it absolutely necessary that the leaders of the Jerusalem church extend some special gesture of goodwill to the Samaritans so that they would not feel themselves to be second-class citizens in the kingdom of God.

Simon Magus was fascinated by the signs that accompanied the giving of the Holy Spirit. It was not long before he betrayed himself. "Sell me the secret," he said in effect. "I'd like to be able to give the Holy Ghost by the laying on of hands."

Peter turned on him in a flash. "Thy money perish with thee. . . . Thou hast neither part nor lot in this matter: for thy heart is not right in the sight of God. . . . thou art in the gall of bitterness, and in the bond of iniquity" (Acts 8:20-23). But Peter did not go beyond reading the innermost secrets of this unregenerate soul. Death had followed the sin of Ananias and Sapphira because they were truly saved and came under apostolic jurisdiction. But Simon Magus was not genuinely saved and Peter left his punishment to God.

Simon Peter exposed the man as an impostor and turned away and left him. Frightened, Simon Magus asked Peter to pray for him. But that was not what the wretched man needed; he needed to pray for himself. If tradition is to be believed, he went back to his sorcery and founded one of the gnostic cults. He is said to have turned up in Rome where he performed his magic tricks even in the court of the caesar.

The events in Samaria made a deep impression on the clan. Peter and John "preached the gospel in many villages of the Samaritans" (Acts 8:25).

As for Philip, God called him away to another task.

II. THE MAN

God is just as interested in individuals as He is in nations. He cared about an Ethiopian eunuch as much as He cared about Samaria.

Any one of the apostles might have had the opportunity of meeting the man from Ethiopia, leading him to Christ, and being instrumental in planting the church in the heart of Africa. But no! The Holy Spirit knew that Peter's and John's hearts were in Jerusalem even while they were touring Samaria. So the Holy Spirit whispered again to Philip the deacon: "Come on, Philip. You and I have an appointment with the secretary of the treasury of the kingdom of Ethiopia."

Responsive as always to the Holy Spirit (one of the qualifications required of a deacon in the Jerusalem church) Philip went off to the desert. He left behind him a flourishing revival. Philip had no question, no quarrel, and no quibble about leaving the limelight to Peter. Philip responded quickly and quietly to the Spirit of God.

So Philip went toward Gaza, to the high road to Egypt. There he waited until on the distant horizon he saw a cloud of dust that soon resolved itself into a group of chariots. They carried the chancellor of the Ethiopian exchequer and his escort.

Like the Samaritans this man stood in a kind of "half relationship" to the nation of Israel. The Samaritans were pagan cousins; the Ethiopian seems to have been a proselyte cousin. He had gone to Jerusalem to worship but apparently he was bitterly disappointed. Possibly he was as disappointed as Martin Luther, who upon arriving at Rome, the city of his dreams, found it full of religious arrogance, pomp, power, and pride and turned from it with disgust and dismay.

We can picture this Ethiopian as he wandered around the city about which he had read and heard so much. Jerusalem was associated with Melchizedek, David, Solomon, and the queen of Sheba! Jerusalem was the city of poets and prophets, the home of the temple, and the heart of a spiritual empire.

No doubt the Ethiopian attended the Jerusalem synagogues and listened to the rules, regulations, and accumulated religious rubbish that the rabbis propounded in the name of God. He probably went to the temple, only to find himself shut out of most of it. The court of the Gentiles would be about as far as he could go and that was more like a mercantile exchange than a sanctuary. He probably wondered, *Why don't the temple authorities clean up this temple traffic?* We can imagine his shock when he discovered that the authorities owned the concessions.

Wandering around the markets of Jerusalem he probably found a shop where portions of the Scriptures were for sale--hand-copied, authorized, and very expensive. Perhaps while browsing through a beautiful copy of the prophecy of Isaiah the word *Ethiopia* caught his eye and he decided to buy it. He could not have made a better choice if he'd asked the chief rabbi himself for advice.

Maybe the Ethiopian heard rumors about the church and went to Annas or Caiaphas with his inquiries. (A man in high social and political position would go to the top.) We can well imagine what kind of answers the high priest and his crowd would have given. And we can wonder why Andrew or Thomas did not lead the Ethiopian to Christ. Perhaps the church avoided him because he was black and a Gentile.

We can speculate that he was sad at heart, empty of soul, and disillusioned as he wandered about the holy city. We know for certain that he went to Jerusalem to worship and that he came away as hungry of heart as when he arrived.

Still seeking, still longing, the Ethiopian headed for home. His entourage arrived first at Gaza and then headed toward Egypt. Ahead of him lay a journey of hundreds and hundreds of miles back to his native land.

When Philip caught up to him, he was reading the prophecy of Isaiah. Although the Ethiopian could not understand what he was reading, he had persevered through fifty-two chapters and was in the middle of the fifty-third. Suddenly he heard a voice that seemed to come from Heaven itself. The speaker must have suspected his bewilderment: "Excuse me, sir. Do you understand what you're reading?" The Ethiopian looked up and saw running alongside his chariot a messenger of God—very earthy and dusty and out-of-breath.

The Spirit had been waiting until this critical moment. Then He had whispered to Philip, "Run, Philip. That's the man, the one in the first chariot, the one reading that book. Run!" Thus the text, the teacher, and the traveler converged on Isaiah 53:7. The Ethiopian was reading these words: "He was led as a sheep to the slaughter; and like a lamb dumb before his shearer, so opened he not his mouth . . . his life is taken from the earth" (as quoted in Acts 8:32-33).

"Of whom speakest the prophet this?" asked the Ethiopian. "Of himself, or of some other man?" (Acts 8:34) Could anyone have asked a more appropriate question? What an opening for a soul-winner. And Philip "began at the same scripture, and preached unto him Jesus" (8:35). Of course he did! Fortunately for the Ethiopian, Philip had not studied at a liberal theological seminary. If he had he would have begun, "Well you see, sir, I subscribe to the deutero-Isaiah hypothesis. Before I can answer your question we must first settle which Isaiah we are talking about."

Thankfully Philip did not expose the inquirer to that kind of high-sounding nonsense. Philip was simply a humble, Bible-believing evangelist. From that magnificent text he led the Ethiopian straight into the arms of Jesus. The preaching of Philip is a classic in personal evangelism.

Philip also instructed the new convert in the first steps of the Christian walk. Philip told the Ethiopian he needed to be baptized now that he had accepted Christ. The Holy Spirit, still in charge, arranged for another of those divine "coincidences" that so often occur in soulwinning: an oasis was nearby. The Ethiopian wasted no time. "See, here is water," he said. "What doth hinder me to be baptized?"

In front of his wondering entourage this high-placed government official stopped his chariot and followed Philip into the water. Having acknowledged the Ethiopian's confession of faith, Philip immersed his illustrious convert.

What happened next is one of those mysteries we will explore with greater understanding when we receive our resurrection bodies and stand with the Ethiopian in Heaven. Then we will hear his testimony from his own lips. For now we can just imagine what he will say.

"I came up out of the water, I rubbed the water from my eyes, and I turned to say something to the man who had appeared out of nowhere, but he wasn't there. He had vanished back into nowhere. I asked my servants, 'Where's that Jewish preacher I picked up a little while back south of Gaza?'

'He seems to have vanished, my lord,' one of them replied. 'Well, he can't have gone far,' I said. 'The country is as flat as a pond. Stand on the high point of the chariot and find out if you can see him.'"

But Philip had vanished. The Holy Spirit gives us the only explanation we will have this side of glory: "The Spirit of the Lord caught away Philip, that the eunuch saw him no more." The Ethiopian, however, had no doubt that God had sent him a special messenger. "He went on his way rejoicing" (Acts 8:39). Meanwhile Philip had been miraculously and instantly transported twenty miles up the coast to the old Philistine city of Ashdod (Azotus).

III. THE PLAN

The divine plan of course was to evangelize the whole Gentile world. The Lord's mandate was to "be witnesses unto me . . . unto the uttermost part of the earth" (Acts 1:8). Nothing could be done about the mandate, however, until the apostles took the divine plan seriously.

The Lord was about to jolt Peter out of his complacency and send him, whether he liked it or not, to the home of a Gentile. Even then the Jerusalem apostles would still be content to drag their feet, but once the door was officially open to Gentiles, the Lord would call and anoint a new apostle—Paul.

In the meantime Philip made tentative attempts at Gentile evangelism himself. He headed up the old Philistine-Phoenician coastline and visited city after city. Ashdod, Lydda, and Joppa were all on his route. On and on he journeyed northward until at last he came to Caesarea.

Caesarea was a bustling modern city with an atmosphere like Rome's. Caesarea was as unlike the sleepy old Palestinian towns as one could imagine. It was the seat of the Roman government in Palestine. An engineering marvel, Caesarea was a bustling seaport. It was the home of the occupying garrison and had such Roman necessities as baths and stadium. The Jews shunned the place like the plague.

Here Philip took up his residence. Long after Peter had come to Caesarea to win Cornelius and his family to Christ, Philip stayed on in this strategic, outward-looking Roman city. Here he brought up his family for God and sought to be a witness for Christ in a thoroughly Gentile atmosphere. He and his family (including four prophetess daughters) were still in Caesarea twenty years later when the great apostle Paul was imprisoned in this city. Paul was attended by his Gentile companion Luke who recorded Philip's story in the book of Acts.

Philip was one man who readily entered into the divine plan to evangelize the whole world. The last glimpse the Holy Spirit gives us of Philip is in Caesarea. The next time we see him we will be in Heaven.

---

1. G. H. Pember, *Earth's Earliest Ages* (Glasgow: Pickering & Inglis, n.d.) 295-299.

10
Cornelius, the Noblest Roman

Acts 10:1–11:18

I. THE ROMAN

II. THE REFUSAL

III. THE REVIVAL

IV. THE REACTION

The conversion of Cornelius is a landmark in world history. At that point in time, divine decree and apostolic action flung open the doors of the church to the great Gentile world that stood beyond the pale of Jewish ritual religion. Until that momentous day the Jews had a virtual monopoly on the things of God. Gentiles had to become Jews in order to participate in the revealed worship of God.

What made matters worse was that the Jews detested the Gentiles and said abominable things about them.[1] The Jews said Gentile idolaters should be cut down with the sword. The Jews said that just as the best kind of serpent was a crushed serpent, so the best kind of Gentile was a dead Gentile. They asserted that of all nations, God loved only Israel. According to the rabbis it was not lawful for a Jew to help a Gentile woman in childbirth because he would be helping to bring another Gentile into the world. If a Jew were to marry a Gentile, from that time forward that Jew was to be considered as dead. Just entering a Gentile house would render a Jew unclean.

A Gentile visiting the Jewish temple in Jerusalem could only go as far as the court of the Gentiles, which was the first and lowest of the various courts. Even there the rabbis showed contempt. They turned that court into a marketplace for buying cattle and changing money.

Beyond the court of the Gentiles was the court of the women, then the court of Israel, and then the court of the priests. Finally, on the highest plane, was the temple. If a Gentile approached the court of the women, he was stopped by a barrier that stood four or five feet high. This barrier was called "the middle wall of partition." Prominent notices displayed on the wall stated in both Greek and Latin that no Gentile was permitted to pass the wall and that the penalty for trespassing was death. Paul himself was nearly torn apart by the Jews because of a false rumor that he had taken a Gentile beyond the barrier.

Naturally the Gentiles responded in kind. They hated and persecuted the Jews. But as far as God was concerned, all difference between Jew and Gentile was abolished and the enmity between Jew and Gentile was removed when Cornelius was converted.

Paul wrote to the Ephesians that in Christ the old enmity is abolished (Ephesians 2:15). Jew and Gentile are made one. There is not a Jewish church and a Gentile church; there is just one church in which all differences of race and caste are forgotten. Before Christ, barriers went up. In Christ, barriers came down, just as the walls of Jericho tumbled before the trumpets of Joshua.

Little did Peter understand the significance of what he did that day when he put his pride and prejudice in his pocket, walked from Joppa to Caesarea, and entered the home of a Gentile soldier to lead him to Christ. Already the Samaritans had been invited into the church. Already an Ethiopian Jewish proselyte had been invited in. Now a full-blooded Gentile and his family were invited in. Soon churches would spring up in Galatia, Corinth, Ephesus, and Rome. The Jewish church headquartered in Jerusalem had tens of thousands of members, but soon Antioch would replace Jerusalem as the center of Christianity, Greek would replace Hebrew as the language of divine revelation, and Gentile Christians would enormously outnumber Jewish Christians.

I. THE ROMAN

In Shakespeare's *Julius Caesar* Antony said of the fallen Brutus: "This was the noblest Roman of them all." Not so! The noblest Roman of them all was a mere centurion named Cornelius. He was stationed on the coast of Palestine at Caesarea, an important seaport built by Herod the Great.

Herod had a long career in creating monuments of magnificent proportions. His trophies included the temple in Jerusalem, the winter palace in Jericho, and the practically impregnable Dead Sea fortress of Masada. His crowning achievement was Caesarea, named in honor of Caesar Augustus.

Herod hoped Caesarea would become a great metropolis rivaling Alexandria in Egypt. Caesarea stood on a direct trade route running east and west from Babylon to Rome. Byzantium was only a twenty-day sail away and Rome itself just two months by sea. Caesarea's layout was the grid plan favored by the Romans. The city contained a forum, baths, offices, temples, houses, villas, and marble statues. A great lighthouse guided ships from afar and an aqueduct brought water from mount Carmel, nine miles away.

Roman engineers had overcome enormous technical difficulties because the site had no natural advantages. It had no coastal bays, headland, or islands to which the harbor could be anchored. The strong current, heavy silting, and rough seas had all posed structural problems. Herod had even used hydraulic concrete, which hardens under water! The magnificent city with its two harbors was a monumental achievement.

Caesarea, with all its paganism and luxury, was the natural capital of Rome in conquered Palestine. Forty-seven miles from Jerusalem, Caesarea was the place where the governor lived. The Jews hated the place. The Romans loved it. It was here that the centurion Cornelius lived.

Cornelius was a noncommissioned officer in the tenth legion of the Roman army. He commanded a special regiment known as the Italian band, a cohort of one thousand men whose duty was to help keep the peace in the province of Palestine. The Italian band was made up of troops drawn exclusively from Italy, and since no provincial troops or mercenaries were in the ranks, this cohort was considered especially reliable. Cornelius, the leader of this privileged regiment, was one of those centurions who were the backbone of the Roman army. They were chosen for their ability to lead men, for their courage, and for their willingness to stand and fight to the last man.

Cornelius was an extraordinary person. He was a devout God-fearing Gentile, though not a Jewish proselyte. Being a proselyte involved circumcision and becoming more or less a Jew. A proselyte was offered admittance to the rites and ordinances of the Jewish religion, but most Gentiles felt that the benefits were not worth the cost. Cornelius was one of those men who were disillusioned by the pagan religions of their day and were greatly attracted to the ethical, moral, and spiritual beliefs of the Jews. But they drew the line at becoming virtually Jews themselves.

The Jews called such people "proselytes of the gate" and sometimes "God-fearers." As far as the Jews were concerned, "God-fearers" were still Gentiles, still outside the covenant, and still aliens to the commonwealth of Israel.

Yet the Holy Spirit speaks highly of Cornelius: "A devout

man, and one that feared God with all his house, which gave much alms to the people, and prayed to God alway" (Acts 10:2). Cornelius had achieved as much as a man of his character, background, training, and ability could achieve, and his name was known in Heaven.

But the Jewish Christians did not seem to care about Cornelius and his fellow Gentiles. In the eight years since Pentecost nobody had come from Jerusalem to tell him, or any member of the Roman garrison, that Jesus had died for sinners on that skull-shaped hill in Jerusalem, that He had been buried, that He had risen from the dead, and that He had ascended to the right hand of the Majesty on high. Nobody had told him that the Holy Spirit had come and the church was being formed. Nobody had told him that the living God of the universe "so loved the world, that he gave his only begotten Son, that whosoever believeth in him should not perish, but have everlasting life" (John 3:16). Peter, James, and John had never bothered with Caesarea. To enter such a place, they reasoned, would be to contaminate themselves. "The uttermost part of the earth" was at their doorstep, yet they had little concern.

So God sent an angel to Cornelius, but He did not commission that angel to preach the gospel to him. (Preaching is our job, not the job of the angels. Had that angel been commissioned to preach the gospel, he would have taken Rome by storm. Soon Britain, Gaul, Parthia, Media, and the ends of the earth would have been reached for Christ. The job would have been completed ten times over in eight years.) God allowed that angel to say but one thing: in essence, "Send for one Simon staying with one Simon" (Acts 10:5-6). And that is exactly what Cornelius did.

II. THE REFUSAL

Simon Peter was staying in the house of Simon the tanner. That fact is significant. The Jews held the trade of the tanner in horror and disgust because it involved handling the skins of dead animals. To touch a dead body under the Levitical ritual code rendered a man ceremonially unclean. By rabbinic law a tanner's house had to be located at least fifty cubits outside a city to decrease the danger of accidental contamination of a devout Jew. If a Jewish girl married a man and found out later that her husband was a tanner, her marriage could be automatically declared null and void. So Simon Peter's prejudices were wearing thin if he could stay with Simon the tanner.

One afternoon Peter announced that he was hungry. His host suggested he retire to the flat roof of the house with its grand view of the Mediterranean and rest while food was being prepared. Peter fell asleep and had the famous vision of the sheet. Down it came from Heaven. The sheet was full of all sorts of creatures pronounced unclean by the Mosaic law: crabs, oysters, shrimp, rabbits, pigs, and all the rest. He heard a voice saying, "Rise, Peter; kill, and eat" (Acts 10:13). Righteously indignant, Peter said, "Not so, Lord; for I have never eaten any thing that is common or unclean" (10:14). G. Campbell Morgan points out that "Not so, Lord" is not a strong enough translation. "Lord, by no means" would be a more accurate rendering. Back came the divine decree: "What God hath cleansed, that call not thou common" (10:15).

The vision occurred three times. Then as Peter rubbed his eyes and tried to decide what the vision meant, the Holy Spirit said to him, "Behold, three men seek thee. Arise therefore, and get thee down, and go with them, doubting nothing: for I have sent them" (Acts 10:19-20). And sure enough there was a knock at the door. His host called up the stairs, "Peter, are you awake? There are three men to see you—Gentiles from Caesarea. One of the soldiers sent them." "Ask them in, Simon," Peter said. "I'm coming right down."

The men had a message and an invitation: "Cornelius the centurion, a just man, and one that feareth God, and of good report among all the nation of the Jews, was warned from God by an holy angel to send for thee into his house, and to hear words of thee" (Acts 10:22).

So that was the meaning of the vision, Peter may have thought. *I must not call Gentiles like Cornelius common or unclean for God has cleansed them. I must go.* It didn't take long for Peter to decide. For the first time in his life he would go to a Gentile city and accept the hospitality of a Gentile home.

It was too late to walk the thirty miles to Caesarea that day so Peter threw caution to the winds. "This," we can hear him say, "is my host, Simon the tanner. I am Simon Peter, an apostle of the Lord Jesus Christ, the Messiah of Israel and the Savior of the world. You fellows had best stay for supper and spend the night here. We'll leave first thing tomorrow morning."

We can imagine too what a lively discussion Peter and his guests had that night. Peter would have asked, "Have you met a man named Philip? He's a friend and colleague of mine. I understand he's living somewhere in Caesarea."

"No sir, we have never heard of the gentleman. Is he a purveyor to the garrison?"

"No, as a matter of fact he's a preacher."

"I wonder why the centurion sent us all the way to Joppa if there's a preacher in town."

"My visit to Cornelius is a much bigger matter than talking to a preacher. This involves a radical departure from anything we have ever done before. This involves opening the door of the church to Gentiles. Until now it has been made up of just Jews. This step calls for the involvement of a prophet and an apostle. Let me tell you about the dream I had this afternoon just about the time you were approaching Joppa . . . "

Perhaps Peter asked questions about Cornelius. Perhaps the men asked questions about Christ. The night must have been far too short for answering all the questions.

Wasting no time, off they went the next day—Peter, the three men, and some Jewish Christians invited by Peter to come along and be impartial witnesses to the historic event that would soon take place in a Gentile city. Significantly, Caesarea faced the Mediterranean sea and looked toward an enormous Gentile world.

III. THE REVIVAL

The centurion treated Peter as though he were more than a man. That is not surprising when we think about it. How many people have ever been given your name and address by an angel? In all the years I have been preaching nobody has ever asked me to come to a meeting because an angel gave him my name and address.

When Peter arrived the house was packed. The word had spread to friends and relatives that Cornelius had seen an angel. *Cornelius?* they may have thought. *The centurion? Surely not. He's not the type. Mrs. Cornelius maybe, but not him. You don't get to be a centurion in the Italian cohort if you're the type that sees angels.*

Peter had an eager and receptive audience. He began by explaining why he, a Jew, was willing to accept an invitation to the home of a Gentile. Then he went straight into the story of Jesus.

Peter's sermon in the house of Cornelius is usually considered to be the draft for Mark's Gospel. The book of Mark was the first of the four Gospels to be written. It was written especially for Romans and reflects the preaching of Peter. Mark's Gospel divides into two parts, as focused by the key verse: "For even the Son of man came not to be ministered unto, but to minister, and to give his life a ransom for many" (Mark 10:45). First we see the Lord Jesus giving His life in *service* and then we see Him giving His life in *sacrifice.*

The message of Mark is just what Peter preached to Cornelius. First Peter spoke of Jesus giving His life in service. "God anointed Jesus of Nazareth with the Holy Ghost and with power: who went about doing good, and healing all that were oppressed of the devil; for God was with him" (Acts 10:38). Then Peter spoke of Jesus giving His life in sacrifice. "Whom they [the Jews and the Gentiles alike] slew and hanged on a tree: Him God raised up the third day, and shewed him openly" (10:39-40).

And then it happened. Revival broke out in that home. The Holy Spirit came down just like at Pentecost. The same signs appeared. God did not send these signs to convince the Gentiles. They needed no convincing. They were ready to believe whatever Peter told them. God sent the signs to convince Peter and the Jewish brothers who accompanied him.

Probably nothing less than this dramatic pouring out of the Holy Spirit on the Gentiles would have convinced the Jerusalem church that it was no longer an exclusive Jewish club. The "middle wall of partition" was broken down. Judaism, even in its Christian form, was obsolete. Gentiles did not have to become Jews in order to become Christians.

But it took the conversion of the apostle Paul, the outbreak of revival in Antioch, the first church conference in Jerusalem, the united testimony of Peter and Barnabas and Paul and James, the writing of the letter to the Galatians, and the writing of the letter to the Ephesians to make the truth begin to sink in. The Jerusalem church was broken up, its people were scattered and deported, the temple was destroyed, and the nation of Israel was dissolved before the truth finally sank in. Judaism was not essential to Christianity; in fact Judaism was a ball and chain around Christianity's leg.

Even to this day some people have the idea that Messianic Jews should have their own separate church in which the various dead forms of Judaism can be observed as part of Christianity. That kind of thinking shows how difficult it is to slay error.

Peter and his friends stayed on at Caesarea for a few days. No doubt he did some sightseeing, but that was not the reason he stayed. He stayed to teach the new Gentile Christians the rudiments of New Testament faith and then he hurried back home.

IV. THE REACTION

While Peter was preaching and teaching and building up the infant Gentile congregation in pagan Caesarea, news filtered back to Jerusalem. (It is amazing how things get around.) One would think that the Jerusalem church would have been delighted to hear what had happened in the home of Cornelius. Not so. The elders in Jerusalem were horrified. They could hardly believe their ears. Peter had disgraced himself, betrayed the church, and practically denied the faith. He had not only gone to the pagan city of Caesarea; he had actually entered a Gentile's house. Worse still, he had taken others with him. Worse yet, he had remained there. Rumor and gossip embellished the story so that by the time Peter came back the Jewish church was ready to excommunicate him.

It says something about the spiritual state of the Jerusalem church that so soon after Pentecost and the great commission the chief apostle could be put on trial for doing exactly what an apostle was supposed to do—what the whole church was supposed to do. He was supposed to preach the gospel to all men everywhere without regard to color, class, or creed. Just because Peter had failed to dot his *i's* and cross his *t's* the way they expected, the Jerusalem believers were outraged. Here was legalism at its worst.

Peter must have been thankful for his independent witnesses as he told the Jerusalem church the story from beginning to end. "The Holy Ghost fell on them, as on us," he said. "What was I, that I could withstand God?" (Acts 11:15,17)

The unbelieving Jewish Christians would never have believed in a thousand years that God could love Gentiles the way He loved Jews if the sign gifts had not followed the baptism of the Holy Spirit in Caesarea. Tongues were a sign to the Jews and in the end they were convinced. Grudgingly they conceded that Peter's preaching to Cornelius was of God, but they didn't like it and they did nothing to follow it up. They sent no missionaries to Caesarea. They did not invite Cornelius to come to Jerusalem and meet the church. But God already had His man in Caesarea. Philip was there to do, as before, what they failed to do.

As for us, we can say, "Peter, we are glad you went to Caesarea. We are glad you met Cornelius. We are glad that a second Pentecost put Cornelius and us on the same spiritual footing before God as you. The Lord knew what He was doing when He enrolled you in the apostolic band."

---

1. Alfred Edersheim, *The Life and Times of Jesus the Messiah* (Grand Rapids: Eerdmans, 1959) I:90-92.

11
Saul of Tarsus, the Greatest Convert

Acts 9:1-31

I. THE MIRACLE OF SAUL'S CONVERSION
  A. The Vigor of His Personality
  B. The Violence of His Persuasion
  C. The Vindictiveness of His Passion
II. THE MANNER OF SAUL'S CONVERSION
  A. A Tremendous Revelation
  B. A Total Revolution
  C. A Typical Resolution
III. THE MEANING OF SAUL'S CONVERSION
  A. Complete the Inspiring of the Word
  B. Commence the Evangelizing of the World

When young Saul of Tarsus had his first taste of blood at the stoning of Stephen, it turned him into a tiger. "Here, you fellows," we can imagine he said to the men who were marching Stephen to the place of execution.

"Put your coats down here. I'll keep an eye on them." Off those coats came, and down they went in a heap at the feet of that imperious young man. "Now then, you fellows, let's see what you can do. Fifty shekels to the man who bounces the first stone off that apostate's head. . . . Well hit, sir. . . . Come on! Hit him again. He's still alive. Listen to the canting hypocrite praying for us. Come on! A hundred shekels to the man who finishes him off."

We can be sure that Stephen will receive a martyr's crown at the judgment seat of Christ. He will be the first in a long and noble lineup of people who washed their robes in the blood of the Lamb and were willing to sacrifice their lives for the cause of Christ. There can be little doubt that Stephen will also receive a soul-winner's crown for the subsequent conversion of Saul, because Saul came away from Stephen's blood-splashed golgotha with three memories embedded deeply in his soul.

First, Saul came away from the stoning of Stephen with some *unforgettable facts*. There is at least a hint in the New Testament that Saul of Tarsus had debated the great truths of the gospel with this keen, Spirit-filled deacon of the Jerusalem church. Let's assume Saul had and imagine what the debate was like.

Saul brought to the encounter a formidable mind, schooled by the brightest teachers of his day. He was a trained rabbi, far ahead of all others in his class. He was the future Gamaliel, perhaps the future high priest of Israel. Saul had the drive, determination, discipline, and dedication required.

He was quite sure that in a debate he could make mincemeat out of Stephen, but Stephen made mincemeat out of Saul. Saul should not have been surprised because he was debating a man full of the Holy Ghost. Saul was up against the Mind that designed the universe, the Mind that inspired Moses, David, Daniel, and Isaiah. Saul was up against the One who wrote all thirty-nine books of the Old Testament and who was busy writing all twenty-seven books of the New Testament. Saul was up against the Holy Spirit.

Stephen looked into Saul's flushed face, straight into his fiery eyes, and said: "But Saul, it behooved Christ to suffer. David said, 'They pierced my hands and my feet.' Of whom did the prophet speak, Saul? Of himself or of some other man? Did not Isaiah say, 'Who hath believed our report? He was led as a lamb to the slaughter'?"

Saul hated what he heard, but he could not gainsay what the Scriptures said. After the debate the stubborn facts of Scripture lay like dormant seeds in his soul. These facts waited like lurking lions in the underbrush of his mind for the moment when they could leap out and tear him to pieces deep inside. He could stone Stephen, but he could not silence Stephen. Even when dead, Stephen still spoke.

Second, Saul came away from the stoning of Stephen with the vision of an *unforgettable faith*. Never could Saul forget Stephen's testimony before the Sanhedrin. Friendless and forsaken, alone in the arena, surrounded by hostile and bitter men, Stephen had been bold under God. The words of his testimony had made the courtroom ring. Stephen's faith embraced the whole Old Testament revelation and he had poured it out like molten lava, heated seven times in the furnace of Calvary. Saul beat his ears with his hands but that noble testimony still rang in his soul. He considered himself to be a man of faith, but his faith was like a cup of tea compared to the vast ocean-fullness of Stephen's faith.

Third, Saul came away from the stoning of Stephen with the memory of an *unforgettable face*. Saul had never seen anyone die looking like an angel. Saul had known that men would die for their faith. He had known that men would die out of fanaticism in spite of the fear that their eyes betrayed. But he had not known anyone could die the way Stephen did. The religious elite of Israel had gnashed on Stephen with their teeth like so many wild animals. Yet the more they had allowed hate and wrath to distort their faces, the more the face of Stephen had shone. It had glowed with the light of another world.

That angel face haunted Saul. It looked at him through the

darkness of his bedroom. It hovered over every landscape. In *Oliver Twist* Charles Dickens told how the face of Nancy haunted Bill Sikes, her murderer, and drove him to a frenzy. Similarly the face of Stephen haunted Saul until it drove him to Jesus. When at last on the Damascus road he saw the face of Jesus, it reminded him of the face of Stephen. Stephen had become so like his Lord that the likeness showed in his very face.

I. THE MIRACLE OF SAUL'S CONVERSION

The conversion of Saul of Tarsus was a miracle of grace that may still be the talk of every quarter and canton of the celestial city.

Imagine for a moment that we are in Jerusalem before Saul's conversion. Here comes a member of the Sanhedrin. Ask him if he thinks Saul will ever become a Christian.

"Saul? Saul of Tarsus become a Christian?" he exclaims. "Why he'd rather eat pork or worship Jupiter!"

Here comes a new widow with her fatherless children. Ask her. The activities of Saul, grand inquisitor of the Sanhedrin, led to her husband's death.

"Saul? Saul of Tarsus become a Christian?" she responds. "It would take a special dispensation of God's grace to make a Christian out of that man, but I pray for him."

But Saul of Tarsus *did* become a Christian in spite of all the obstacles of birth, breeding, background, belief, and behavior. He became a Christian in spite of the vigor of his personality, the violence of his persuasion, and the vindictiveness of his passion.

A. The Vigor of His Personality

Some people are pliable and easily molded, but not Saul. His personality was hewn out of rock—he was all granite and iron. He would not even bow to the established party line, though it was enunciated by his teacher and mentor Gamaliel.

"Leave them alone lest you end up fighting against God" was Gamaliel's advice. *Nonsense!* thought Saul. *Coexist with Christianity? With all due respect, Gamaliel is getting old and soft.*

Saul was hard as a diamond, inflexible and adamant. He summoned all the power of his forceful personality for the fight ahead. He summoned all the flaming fervor of his natural eloquence, all the thundering energy of his being, all the drive of his unbridled will. He became a pulsating engine of destruction. No Alexander, Caesar, or Napoleon ever outshone Saul of Tarsus in dynamism and determination. All his mind, soul, heart, and strength were set ablaze by his hatred for Jesus and the detested cult of the Nazarene.

B. The Violence of His Persuasion

Saul had his own convictions about the Christ of God and what kind of a Messiah He would be. The meek and lowly Jesus of Nazareth was certainly no Messiah according to Saul's book. Jesus was nothing but a weak and watery impostor.

Saul envisioned a militant Messiah—a true son of David, a man of war. The Messiah would smite the power of Rome and make Jerusalem the capital of a new world empire founded on the Mosaic law in accordance with the sayings of the prophets.

Saul was looking for a martial Messiah, not a meek Messiah. The very expression *meek Messiah* was a contradiction in terms. Saul wanted a Messiah who would let Himself be crowned, not a Messiah who would let Himself be crucified. Saul wanted a Messiah who came to reign, not a Messiah who came to redeem.

The thought of Calvary was revolting. That scene should not be the grand finale of the Messiah's sojourn on this planet. The idea that great David's greater Son should come but end up being crucified by the Romans was preposterous!

Saul knew his Bible. He knew by heart the Scripture "Cursed is every one that hangeth on a tree" (Galatians 3:13; Deuteronomy 21:23). That God's Son should hang on a tree was utterly ridiculous. Worse, it was blasphemy. Away with anyone who preached such outrageous heresy! With Saul of Tarsus it was no matter for mere discussion and debate.

C. The Vindictiveness of His Passion

Saul nursed in his soul such a fierce hatred of Christianity that he offered himself to the Sanhedrin as their grand inquisitor, their Torquemada, their licensed instrument to stamp out this heretical cult. The wealthy aristocratic men who ran the Sanhedrin were only too glad to have their dislike of Jesus of Nazareth confirmed by the fiery eloquence of young Saul and to have someone do their dirty work for them. They gave him a mandate and a free hand.

In later years Saul himself said wonderingly that he had been "exceedingly mad" against the Christians (Acts 26:11). Acts 8:3 says that he "made havock of the church" and Greek scholars tell us that no stronger metaphor could have been used. It was used in classical Greek to describe the ravages of a wild boar uprooting a vineyard. This metaphor occurs nowhere else in the New Testament.

Saul had one controlling passion. It drove sleep from his eyes and mastered all other passions and lusts. He wanted to beat, brand, bully, and bludgeon every man, woman, boy, and girl who named the name of Christ. He was in just such a mood when he was racing toward Damascus the day he was saved.

Saul's attendants on the road to Damascus must have cursed him underneath their breath. At high noon when the merciless Syrian sun beat down from a brazen sky, any sensible man would stop by the side of the road, find shade and shelter beneath some palm trees, and have some lunch and a refreshing siesta. But Saul was driven on by his hate. He was like a man possessed. He was in a fever of rage and was afraid that someone would get to Damascus before him and spread the word that he was coming. He couldn't bear the thought that some of his enemies might escape.

So the salvation of Saul of Tarsus was a miracle. He was saved when humanly speaking everything was against his being converted. He was saved in spite of the vigor of his personality, in spite of the violence of his persuasion, and in spite of the vindictiveness of his passion. He was saved even though he could not be reached with reasoning—one cannot reason with a man who knows he's right, who is as stubborn as a mule, and who is driven by a burning hate. Saul's conversion was nothing less than a miracle.

Actually, every conversion is a miracle. That someone born in sin, shaped in iniquity, blind to the truth of God, deaf to the gospel, dead to the Son of God, and determined to go his own way should come face to face with the risen Christ and enthrone Him as Savior and Lord is a miracle indeed. It is a miracle that happens hundreds of times every day.

II. THE MANNER OF SAUL'S CONVERSION

Some souls seem to be born gradually into the kingdom of God. Others seem to be hurled in headfirst. For some the light dawns so slowly they can never say for sure exactly when they were saved. For others the light dawns like a lightning flash and the truth penetrates like a thunderclap. When Saul was saved, there was a burning voice and a blinding vision and all of a sudden he was prostrate in the dust confessing his newfound faith.

A. A Tremendous Revelation

In all his later writings Saul hardly ever referred to the human life of Jesus of Nazareth. Saul first saw Him, first knew Him, and first enthroned Him as "the Lord from heaven" (1 Corinthians 15:47). Ever afterwards that was how he thought of Jesus.

"Who art thou, Lord?" Saul cried. "I am Jesus whom thou persecutest," the Lord replied (Acts 9:5). At once Saul's world collapsed like a house of cards. His religion was useless.

Saul was a circumcised Jew, a Benjamite, a Hebrew of the Hebrews, a Pharisee, a firebrand of the Jewish faith, a moral man, and a law-abiding citizen. He observed the rites of religion and performed the deeds of the law, but his every thought had been sinful. All his religion had done for him was make him an active enemy of Christ. It had simply confirmed him in his sins and persuaded him he did not need a Savior. As a religious man he felt no need to confess his sin and accept Christ as Savior.

What a tremendous revelation it was to Saul that he was lost and undone and on his way to a Christless eternity. He realized he was the enemy of the gospel and the committed foe of the living, risen, ascended Son of the living God. Without such conviction of sin no religious man can ever hope to be saved.

B. A Total Revolution

One moment Saul of Tarsus was the chief of sinners; the next moment he was a devout believer with his feet set on the road to becoming the chief of saints. One moment he thought Jesus of Nazareth to be an impostor; the next moment he owned Him as Lord and God. One moment he was a terrorist committed to the ruthless extermination of the church; the next moment he was a new creature in Christ Jesus. In Acts 9:1 he was breathing out threats; in Acts 9:11 the Lord said, "Behold, he prayeth."

There was a total revolution within Saul. He was changed in a moment, in the twinkling of an eye. He did not go through a long drawn-out process of psychological reconditioning. He experienced *conversion:* a life-transforming change that affects the mind, heart, will, conscience, body, soul, and spirit.

C. A Typical Resolution

"Lord," Saul said, "What wilt thou have me to do?" (Acts 9:6) Before his conversion Saul had served the Sanhedrin; now he wanted to serve the Savior. He knew that "faith without works is dead" (James 2:26). Saul resolved from that day forward he would allow no rivals, no refusals, no retreat. Jesus would be Lord of every thought and action. (Sooner or later every genuine born-again believer must acknowledge in some measure the sovereignty of the Spirit of God in his life.)

So Saul of Tarsus was already well on the way to becoming the great apostle Paul. Within a decade the world was going to hear from this man. He was an apostle "born out of due time" (1 Corinthians 15:8) but he would come "not a whit behind the very chiefest apostles" (2 Corinthians 11:5).

III. THE MEANING OF SAUL'S CONVERSION

What does a newly saved person do? To a large extent it depends on the person. We probably would have said: "The best thing for you to do, Saul, is to go to Jerusalem and attend the services of the church and learn all you can about the Christian life. There are some good Bible teachers there like Peter and John. You can learn a lot from them."

Well that is just what Saul did *not* do. He decided to get away from people altogether. He needed time to think, read his Bible, and pray. So off he went toward the silences of Sinai—to Horeb, the mount where God had met with Moses. Saul dropped out of sight for a number of years until even his name was thankfully forgotten by the persecuted saints of God.

Saul, however, was not forgotten by God. He was in God's school. His teacher was the Holy Spirit and his text-book was the Bible. God was preparing him for the greatest of all ministries, second only to that of his beloved Lord from Heaven.

Saul, God said, "is a chosen vessel unto me" (Acts 9:15). God had built into him a combination of qualifications He had not built into any of the other believers in the ever-growing Christian community. Saul was a Jew, a Roman, and a Greek. He was a Jew by birth, training, religion, and education. He was a Greek by scholarship, learning, and language. He was a Roman by citizenship—free-born. Saul of Tarsus was cosmopolitan, a man made for the world. With the conversion of such a uniquely qualified man, the time had come for God to complete the inspiring of the Word and commence the evangelizing of the world.

A. Complete the Inspiring of the Word

There were new truths to be conveyed to men. Saul was the man for the job. He was an intellectual giant with a mind commensurate to the task. A major part of the Bible had not yet been written and Saul was chosen to write it. God needed a man with his genius, boldness, and authority.

When Saul of Tarsus departed for Arabia, the Christian vocabulary did not yet exist. Words like *Adam, Moses, law, sin, death, grace, works, atonement, redemption, adoption, justification, faith,* and *righteousness* existed in the general vocabulary of the Hebrew people. But such words had not yet attained their full stature in Christ. Words inspired by the Holy Spirit came to the mind of Saul when he was in Arabia. He later wrote, "I conferred not with flesh and blood" (Galatians 1:16). Saul took Genesis, Leviticus, Psalms, and Isaiah in his backpack when he went into the wilderness. He returned with Romans, Ephesians, and Thessalonians in his heart.

B. Commence the Evangelizing of the World

There were new tribes to be converted to God. Saul of Tarsus was the man for that task too.

When Saul was saved, the church was exclusively Jewish. When he died, churches dedicated to the worship of Jesus existed in every major city of the Roman empire. Gentiles had poured into the church in a living tide. Saul had taken the pagan world by storm.

When Saul was saved, Jerusalem was the geographic center of the Christian world. Peter, James, and John were the pillars of the church. When Saul died, Rome was the center of the Christian world and Jerusalem had become a mere suburb. An unimportant center on the backwaters of history, Jerusalem would soon be wiped off the map for centuries.

What was the meaning of Saul's conversion? His experience on the Damascus road was a major turning point in the history of mankind. Every conversion is intended to be just such a turning point. The conversion of men like Martin Luther, William Carey, David Livingstone, D. L. Moody, and the like have all been high-water marks in the history of this planet. God intends that your conversion and mine should be the same. May each of us make sure it is.

12
Paul,
the Ablest Missionary

Acts 28:30-31

I. HOW PAUL REVIEWED THE PAST
   A. His Unregenerate Past
   B. His Unrecorded Past
   C. His Unrivaled Past
II. HOW PAUL REDEEMED THE PRESENT
III. HOW PAUL REGARDED THE FUTURE

The book of Acts ends with Paul in prison in Rome. His terms of imprisonment appear to be light, as would befit the detention of a Roman citizen. He was chained to a soldier and probably he could not come and go as he pleased, but he was free to receive any visitors he wished.

We can visualize the great apostle running his house like the courtroom of a king. Correspondence flowed in from all over the empire. A constant stream of visitors came and went. His attendants, including his beloved physician, executed his decisions. There was no pomp or ceremony; Paul had no use for that kind of thing. But even the most disinterested jailer must have been impressed by the power, influence, and diligence of this extraordinary Jew who possessed Roman citizenship, spoke flawless Greek, and wrote words that commanded greater respect than those of the emperor.

Paul was permitted to live in his own rented house. We are going to spend some time with him there. We are going to picture how he reviewed the past, redeemed the present, and regarded the future. We will see a man who had few regrets (and all those under the blood), who was wholly committed to a single cause, and who was quite unafraid of the days ahead.

I. HOW PAUL REVIEWED THE PAST

Everyone has a past. It must be a good feeling to be comfortable with one's past. We can do nothing about the past except applaud it or apologize for it. What has been done has been done and can never be undone. Only God can do anything about the sinful past. He promises to blot it out. He promises even more. He says He can restore the years that the locusts have eaten (Joel 2:25).

As we picture Paul reviewing his life we think of his unregenerate past, his unrecorded past, and his unrivaled past.

A. His Unregenerate Past

Paul was raised by devout Jewish parents in the port city of Tarsus on the coast of Asia Minor. His father was a Roman citizen. How he acquired this priceless honor we are not told. Most likely a Roman general or administrator in southeastern Asia Minor granted citizenship to him for rendering some valuable service. The service may have been rendered to Pompey or Mark Antony. As Roman citizens Paul's family must have associated with the cream of society in Tarsus and Cilicia, even though their strict observance of Jewish law made it impossible for them to exploit their advantages fully.

Paul described himself as a Hebrew of the Hebrews—a Hebrew sprung from Hebrews (Philippians 3:5). He was proud of his heritage as a Jew and of his status as a Roman. He grew up in a bustling seaport thronged with sailors and merchants from all over the known world. A cosmopolitan Hellenist and Greek-speaking Jew, he was also a trained rabbi for he sat at the feet of Gamaliel. That in itself set Paul apart from the rank and file, even among the Jews.

Gamaliel, the grandson of the illustrious rabbi Hillel, was a Pharisee. His learning was so great that he was one of only seven doctors of Jewish law who were given the title *rabban*. Upon his death this proverb was circulated among the Jews: "Since Rabban Gamaliel died the glory of the law has ceased." They were wrong of course. They would have been more correct to say, "Since the Lord Jesus died the glory of the law has ceased."

At the feet of this distinguished teacher young Paul imbibed his views of Judaism. Already the first shoots of the Talmud were flourishing, and a Jewish student being taught by a learned rabbi would learn more about the Midrash and the Mishna than about the Bible.

Paul of course memorized all 613 commandments of the Mosaic law. But he was even more conversant with the work of Hillel, who brought to full flower the system of exegesis that applied Greek reasoning to the Hebrew Scriptures. He knew by heart all the intricate rules, regulations, teachings, and traditions that the Jews had hedged around the law. For instance, young Paul had at his fingertips all the dos and don'ts with which the Jews tried to protect the sabbath. (Christ swept all these rules away as so much high-sounding nonsense.)

Yet this star pupil—brilliant, sincere, protected, privileged, and promoted—later wrote the word *ignorant* over that early period of his life. Ignorance was his only excuse for his rabid persecution of the church. "I did it ignorantly," he said (1 Timothy 1:13).

Paul was totally ignorant of the law of God all the time he

studied it in those days. He played with it as a child plays with an ornament. No one—father, mother, schoolmaster, or fellow student—ever took the Sword out of its sheath to show him its glittering edge, its divine workmanship, and its ability to pierce the conscience, stab the soul, and bring fearful conviction of sin. Gamaliel taught those eager young men who thronged his academy what Rabbi So-and-So said and what Rabbi Such-and-Such said. Gamaliel so distorted, dissected, and dissipated the Word of God that by the time Paul graduated, the Sanhedrin had marked him as the young man most likely to succeed. The church had marked him as the young man most likely to persecute Christians.

A persecutor is what Paul became. He made havoc of the church. He cheered those who stoned Stephen and held their coats. He obtained warrants from Caiaphas and Annas and persecuted the church at home and abroad with a single-mindedness and savagery that struck terror into the hearts of Christians everywhere.

Paul's later words reveal a deep pang of remorse: "I persecuted this way unto the death, binding and delivering into prisons both men and women. . . . I imprisoned and beat in every synagogue them that believed. . . . when they were put to death, I gave my voice against them. . . . [I] compelled them to blaspheme. . . . beyond measure I persecuted the church of God, and wasted it" (Acts 22:4,19; 26:10-11; Galatians 1:13).

How Paul thanked God after his conversion for the precious blood of Christ. All his sins against the Christians were under the blood. God forgave his sins and forgot them, but Paul could not forgive himself nor could he forget. The faces of men, women, boys, and girls rose up to haunt him. At night he would see faces, hear voices, and wake up bathed in cold sweat—even after he had been saved for years and those sins had been cast behind God's back, buried in the depth of the sea, and blotted out as by a cloud.

No wonder Paul had such a burden for the poor saints of Jerusalem. No wonder he took collections for them everywhere he went. No wonder he begged and pleaded with his Gentile converts in city after city to contribute funds for the needy Christians in Jerusalem. Many of them he had widowed, orphaned, and beggared. Their faces were ever before him even though God had eternally banished his sins from His mind and memory.

B. His Unrecorded Past

With constant delight the great apostle remembered that never-to-be-forgotten experience on the Damascus road, the startling heavenly vision of the risen ascended Christ. How that experience colored all his thinking ever afterwards! Paul had never known Jesus during the days of His flesh; he knew Him only as "the Lord from heaven" (1 Corinthians 15:47). That blinding vision was the beginning of his understanding of the great commission. "Once I was blind, but now I can see," he must often have said.

The Holy Spirit draws the veil of silence over the next few years in Paul's life. But the new convert was not wasting his time. In Arabia under the guidance of the Holy Spirit Paul formulated the theology of the New Testament. Those years in Arabia were essential for him to sort out fact from rabbinical fable. He had so much to unlearn. Much of the teaching he had received from Gamaliel was worthless to him in his new life in Christ.

During this silent period Paul seems to have been disinherited by his family (Philippians 3:8 says that he "suffered the loss of all things") and he had already received the "mighty ordination of the nail-pierced hands" for his work among the Gentiles (Acts 9:15), so there was nothing to stop him from getting busy for God. Paul was not the kind of man to sit around waiting for a call from the Jerusalem church—they were glad he was somewhere else. Paul, saved or unsaved, was trouble as far as the Christians in Jerusalem were concerned.

As Paul reviewed his past he remembered his first visit to Jerusalem after his conversion. He remembered the incredible loneliness he felt. The whole church eyed him with the greatest suspicion. They thought he was simply pretending to be saved to worm his way into the congregations in Jerusalem as a Sanhedrin spy and informer. Then Barnabas, a true son of consolation, befriended him and introduced him to the apostles.

Paul looked back with pleasure on the time he spent in Jerusalem with Peter. "Here's the upper room, brother Paul," he could hear Peter saying. "Here's where Jesus entered into Jerusalem to the hallelujahs and hosannas of the crowd. Here's where He overturned the tables of the money-changers. Here's where we all went to sleep while He wept and prayed over yonder. Here's where I denied Him, to my shame."

God warned Paul that Jerusalem was a dangerous place for him, yet he felt drawn to it. Ultimately events there led to his imprisonment. He spent years of his life in prison at Caesarea and Rome, thanks to the thoughtlessness of the Jerusalem church.

C. His Unrivaled Past

Paul remembered when the real call came. First the Antioch church needed a teacher, and his friend Barnabas came to recruit him for that ministry. Then the Antioch church needed a missionary, and Paul and Barnabas with young Mark in tow set out to evangelize the regions beyond.

Paul thought of his years as a missionary. There was his first missionary journey to Cyprus and the thrilling confrontation with Elymus the sorcerer and the conversion of Sergius Paulus, the island's Roman governor.

Then the great Taurus range beckoned to him to return to Cilicia where he had already labored for years on his own. Taking a firm hold on the leadership of the missionary team, he announced his decision: "We'll head north, pass through the Cilician gates, and then travel on into Galatia. Danger? What's the matter with you, John Mark? If we're in the will of God, so what if there's danger? There's danger everywhere. You're quitting? Well, my young friend, all I can say is that you have a great deal to learn about discipleship."

Paul conducted evangelistic campaigns in Pisidian Antioch, Iconium, Lystra, and Derbe. A pattern soon developed. Paul's policy was to go to the Jews of the local synagogue first. Inevitably the synagogue divided right down the middle. The unbelieving Jews were bitterly hostile. Rage, jealousy, blasphemy, and persecution always followed.

Paul remembered being hailed as a god at Lystra one moment and being stoned as a troublemaker the next. *It was just as well that John Mark went home,* Paul thought. How he valued dear patient Barnabas, always willing to play second fiddle. He never complained and was willing to suffer with Paul for the cause of Christ.

Paul remembered the joy of planting churches everywhere. Hundreds of people became Christians, were baptized, and learned the rudiments of the gospel and sound exegesis of the Old Testament. Going back to ordain elders was a wonderful memory also.

Then came the Jerusalem conference and his confrontation with the Jewish church over the freedom of Gentile Christians from the law of Moses, from circumcision, from sabbath-keeping, and from Israel's dietary laws. Even in prison as Paul sat reminiscing, he could not hold back a grateful *Amen!* for God's sovereign overruling of that conference. It was still hard to believe that Peter and the ascetic, legalistic, narrow-minded James took his side. He would have liked to free Jews as well as Gentiles from the bondage of the law, but God would take care of that in His own time. Paul was sure the destruction of the temple, foretold by Jesus, would help.

Paul thought also of his next two missionary journeys. The disagreement with Barnabas over John Mark was sad, but God stepped in and provided Silas, Timothy, Titus, and a host of other young men to take Barnabas's place. Paul went back to Galatia and on to Troas.

Then God overruled again. Paul met the man from Macedonia, first in vision and then in the flesh as dear Dr. Luke walked into his life to confirm Paul's call to evangelize Europe.

Memories arose: Philippi and the jail; Thessalonica and revival; Berea and a people zealous to test all teaching by the Book; Athens and the once-in-a-lifetime opportunity to speak for God on Mars hill. *How strange that the Greeks could be so brilliant in philosophy, politics, art, and science and be so blind in religion,* Paul mused.

When Paul traveled on to Corinth and Ephesus, hundreds of thousands of people found Christ. Paul planted church after church in city after city in country after country. Almost single-handedly, in cooperation with the Spirit of God, he evangelized all the Eastern European Mediterranean. What a life he had lived since Jesus came into his heart. The soldier chained to his wrist suddenly awoke as Paul shouted, "Hallelujah!"

II. HOW PAUL REDEEMED THE PRESENT

We picture Paul looking at his prayer book. It listed so many places and so many people. Barnabas, Mark, Timothy, Titus, Priscilla, Aquila, Aristarchus, Apollos, Rufus, Alexander, Demas, Crispus—name after name was listed. Paul thought of the hundreds of men he had discipled. Now in the ministry, they were blazing gospel trails to vast regions beyond. Paul's prayer list was enough to keep him busy from morning to night.

He was praying for others too: Lydia; the Philippian jailer and his wife and children; the poor little slave girl; Alexander the coppersmith; Festus; Felix; King Agrippa; that poor lost man known to the world as Nero Claudius Caesar Augustus Germanicus; the soldiers; and the members of the praetorian guard, many of whom he had already won to Christ.

Reminded of the soldier chained to him, Paul said, "Tell me, my friend, you're new to the guard, aren't you? Where are you from? Are you married? Two little boys, eh! What are their names? Tell me, Marcus, has anyone ever told you about Jesus? Let me tell you how I met Him."

We picture Paul witnessing, praying, and redeeming many long hours by writing letters. While sitting in his rented house he carried on a voluminous correspondence. Some of his letters have been preserved. No greater letters have ever been written than Paul's prison letters to the Ephesians, the Philippians, the Colossians, and Philemon. Paul wrote these letters under the direct control of the Holy Spirit. They are God-breathed, inerrant, divinely inspired, and part of the living fabric of the Word of God. They will outlast all the suns and stars in space. These jewels of inspiration will dwell in our minds for the endless ages of eternity.

Much happened to Paul between the time he wrote his Epistle to the Romans from Corinth and the time he wrote his Epistle to the Ephesians from Rome. He called at Philippi and Ephesus on his way to Jerusalem. He warned the Ephesian elders that heresy was on the prowl and that they were responsible for the flock. He brought to Jerusalem a magnificent financial gift from the Gentile churches of the West. He was conned into going into the temple court to prove his Jewishness. He was beaten up by the mob and rescued by the Roman garrison. He addressed the multitude and then the Sanhedrin. Because a conspiracy to murder him was afoot he was hurried off to the Roman city of Caesarea. There he lingered in jail for two long years. He appeared before Felix, Festus, and King Agrippa. In exasperation Paul appealed to caesar and now the apostle was in Rome, where he languished in prison.

The wheels of justice creaked on just as slowly in Rome as they did everywhere else. However, Paul faced an added element of danger. He now realized that it was well within the bounds of possibility that he would be executed. When he had appealed to caesar in A.D. 59 there were no indications that Nero would degenerate into a monster. But by A.D. 62 the official attitude toward Christians had changed. Nero's wise tutor Seneca was retired. The Jewess Poppaea wound the imperial tyrant around her little finger. The corrupt Tigellinus had Nero's ear. In just two years Nero would set fire to Rome and blame the Christians for the holocaust.

Through all that happened between the writing of the Epistle to the Romans and the writing of the Epistle to the Ephesians, Paul grew to the full measure of his stature in Christ. His letters from prison had a new emphasis on the lordship of Christ and on the mystery of the church and its relationship to Christ.

So we picture Paul redeeming the present by writing, by witnessing, and by interceding. The past was past. The future was future. He had today. He saw to it that each passing moment was freighted with precious cargo to be weighed in for reward at the judgment seat of Christ.

III. HOW PAUL REGARDED THE FUTURE

Paul never worried about the future. Whenever he tried to lift the veil and peer into the future, all he could see was Christ. The Lord Jesus dominated his horizon.

If caesar should set him free, then for him to live was Christ. He would evangelize Spain. Beyond Spain were Northern Europe, the Germanic tribes across the Danube, and the Angles on the tiny island of Britannia. If Nero set him free, Paul would fling himself into global evangelism with a passion and a purpose that would make the past seem like wasted time.

If Nero were to command his execution, then hallelujah! To die would be gain. He would be absent from the body and present with the Lord.

Paul already had one glimpse of glory. He was caught up into the third heaven and saw things untranslatable. He could never decide afterwards if he had been in the body or out of the body during that experience. All he knew was that the experience was real, tangible, and audible—what lay beyond the grave was as solid as what lay on this side. What he saw and sensed over there filled him with "a desire to depart, and to be with Christ; which is far better" (Philippians 1:23).

The word Paul used for *desire* in writing to the Philippians is the usual word for *lust* in the New Testament. Indeed the original word is translated "lust" some thirty times. Paul was lusting to go to Heaven. He tasted the powers of the world to come and became an addict of glory. Let Nero execute him. All Nero could do was promote him to glory. Paul's future would be Jesus! Paul's future would be forever. His future would be "joy unspeakable and full of glory" (1 Peter 1:8). Neither caesar nor the Sanhedrin nor Satan could rob Paul of his future. His future would be glorious.

In the end Paul witnessed before Nero, and Nero had him executed. But when Paul arrived in glory, Jesus had him crowned.